Digital
Command Control

Ian Morton

Ian Allan
PUBLISHING

First published 2007
Reprinted 2007

ISBN (10) 0 7110 3152 5
ISBN (13) 978 0 7110 3152 4

Published by Ian Allan Publishing

an imprint of Ian Allan Publishing Ltd, Hersham, Surrey KT12 4RG.
Printed by Ian Allan Printing Ltd, Hersham, Surrey KT12 4RG.

Code: 0708/A1

Visit the Ian Allan Publishing web site at: www.ianallanpublishing.com

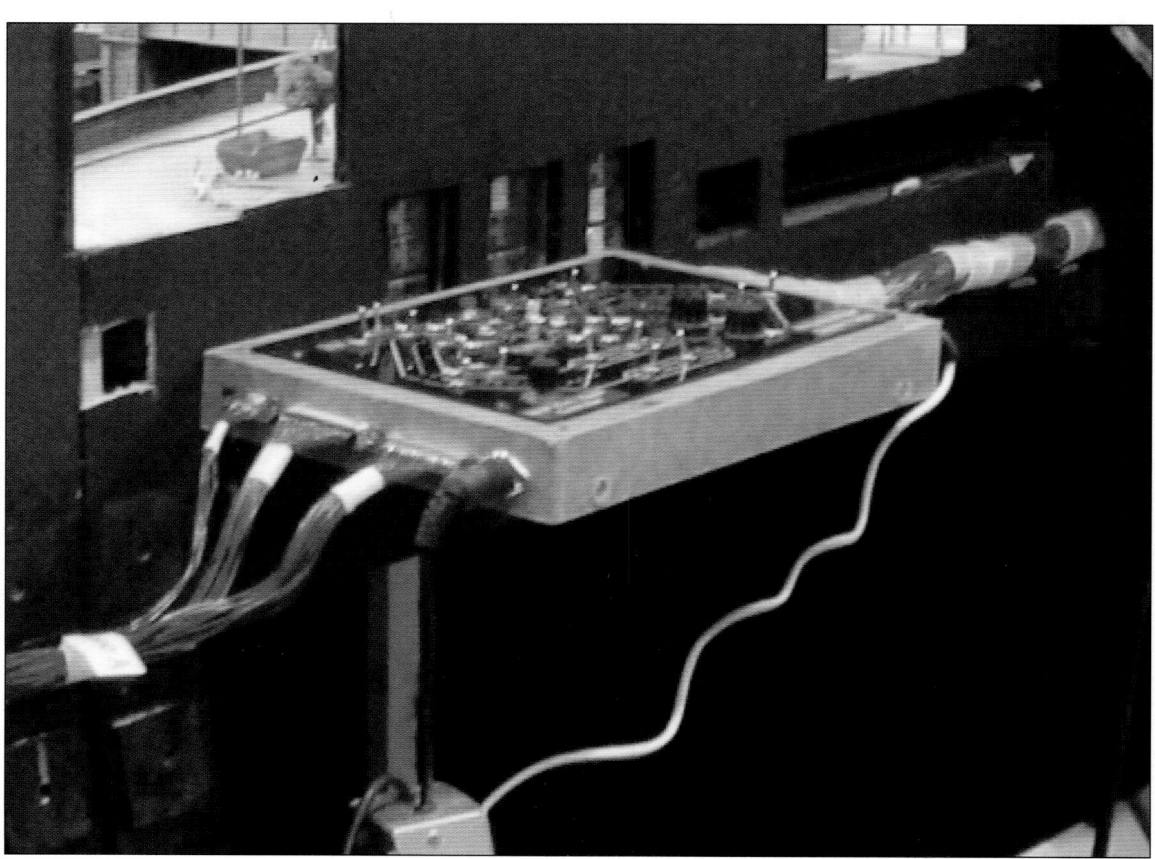

RIGHT: *With multiple controllers, various track sections and electrically operated points and signals, the amount of wiring needed for conventional control of a model railway can reach staggering proportions. This is the control panel and associated cabling behind Kier Hardy's Wibdenshaw layout. DCC can reduce substantially the amount of wire and controls needed to operate a model railway.*
Picture: Kier Hardy
www.kierhardy.co.uk

Contents

Foreword

Digital Command Control has generated much discussion and comment amongst railway modellers. You will find people who are passionately in favour of it and others so vehemently opposed to it that you would think it had been invented by Dr. Beeching himself. Much of the debate has taken place without the benefit of facts or evidence and in this respect I hope that this volume can at least shed a little light on the proceedings.

Whilst I have no axe to grind either for, or against, DCC I have observed its development, and that of many of the command control systems that preceded it. The current debate has all the hallmarks of the two-rail versus three-rail arguments of the 1950s and, I suspect, the clockwork versus electric confrontation from even further back.

Everyone needs to make up their own mind about DCC. For those with a large layout or massive collection of locomotives the cost of conversion may seem too high. For those with more modest aspirations the same may also seem true. For those just entering, or coming back to, the hobby the choice is much easier. It all comes down to the question of what DCC can do for you.

For a young child's train set a simple DCC system, such as Bachmann's E-Z Command controller can make connecting up and operation easier than ever before. For a single engine shunting layout it would be far more a matter of personal choice.

Scale and gauge are not bars to using DCC. Locomotives from Z through to Gauge 1 and above have successfully been fitted with decoders and just about every possible variation of 4mm scale has been DCC equipped from P4 to 009.

Despite what many of its opponents may say, in most cases a DCC layout is easier to wire up than an equivalent conventional layout and DCC equipped locomotives perform better than the same locomotive on conventional control. On the other hand some people will never need the extra functionality that DCC offers. But, once you have read the contents of this book at least you will have the information to make the decision about whether DCC is right for you and, if it is, how to select and install the system that best meets your needs.

I should add that the use of a model railway in these pages to illustrate an idea does not imply that the layout shown is DCC operated. The pictures have been chosen to explain what DCC can do for you. Finally I should like to thank those who have provided photographs and information and my family for letting me spend so many uninterrupted hours bashing away at the computer keyboard.

Happy modelling.

Ian Morton,
December 2006

Introduction to DCC

When operating a model railway most people want to feel that they are driving a locomotive.

On a conventional model railway if you want to have more than one locomotive on the track at any one time then you need to provide isolated track sections to store the locomotives that you are not using so that they don't move when you turn the controller on. If you wish to operate more than one locomotive at a time it starts to get complicated as you now need a controller for each locomotive, connected to electrically separate sections of track. You also need to be able to select which sections of track are connected to each controller.

Even on a simple layout the wiring involved with multiple controllers, section switches and isolating switches can become complex and confusing. Of course once you have installed and sorted out any problems with the wiring you then have to learn how to operate it all.

Despite all the time, effort and expense involved in setting your conventional control system up you will still find that before you can drive the train you will have to do a lot of work switching the track power. Common railway activities like double-heading, banking or parking engines next to each other are all difficult to achieve due to the inflexibility of the system.

For years modellers have put up with these limitations or created involved methods to get around them but now there is a better way. The computer 'chip' has invaded every area of life and model railways are no exception.

The technology is called Digital Command Control, normally abbreviated to DCC. Using this technology it is possible to run as many locomotives as you wish on your layout without having to worry about selecting which track is connected to which controller or worrying about where the isolated sections are to park your locomotive. All you need to do is choose a locomotive and drive it.

Even better, the system is simple to install and operate; it requires less technical knowledge than wiring up a conventional system.

Despite this there are many myths and misconceptions surrounding DCC. Once you actually take the plunge you will find that there is nothing to be scared of.

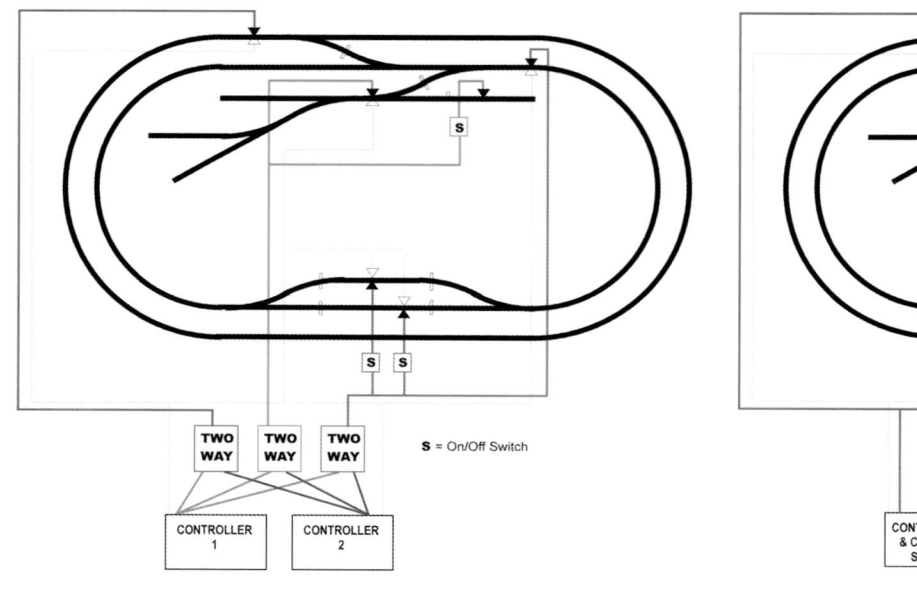

S = On/Off Switch

TWO WAY	TWO WAY	TWO WAY

CONTROLLER 1	CONTROLLER 2

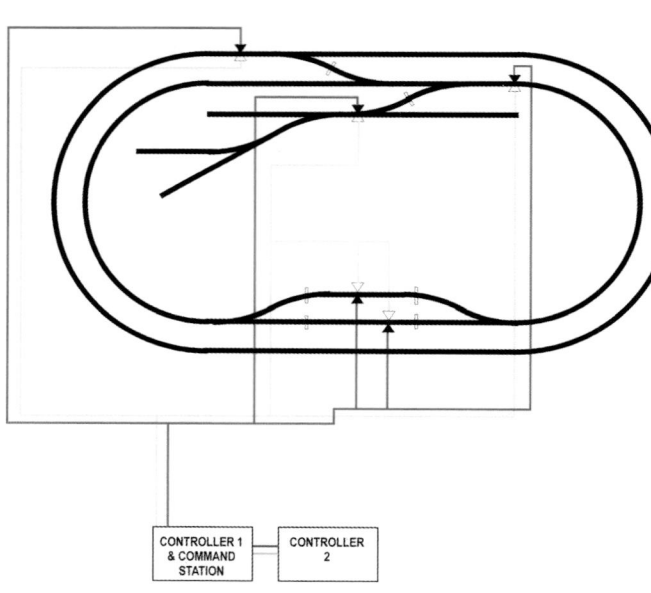

CONTROLLER 1 & COMMAND STATION	CONTROLLER 2

Controller

Controller sends settings to Command Station

Command Station

Command Station sends Digital Signal to Booster

Booster

Booster sends Digital Signal and Power to Track

Decoder reads Digital Signal and uses Power to Drive Motor

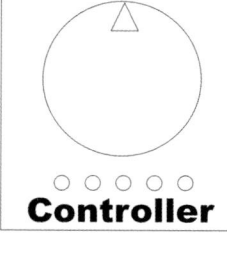

Locomotive with Decoder

Track

The Myths and Misconceptions

It's expensive.
Well, yes it is if you are trying to convert a medium or large layout and matching locomotive stud all at once. It would be far better to phase DCC operation in or, if you really must do it all at once, save up for it.

The decoders are difficult to fit.
They can be. Small locomotives, such as N scale saddle-tanks, can be difficult. Vintage commercial products with live metal chassis can also cause problems, as can kit and scratchbuilt steam locos but in many cases there is a workaround. There are very few models where it really is impossible to fit a DCC decoder.

DCC won't work with certain types of point.
Simply not true. DCC is more sensitive to short circuits so if you have a problem with incorrectly wired or built points or wildly out of gauge wheelsets that cause a short going over pointwork then DCC will highlight the problem. The fault lies with your wiring or wheels and ought to be corrected anyway.

DCC needs special wiring.
Not true. Whilst you may wish to put special wiring in you can replace a conventional controller on your layout with a DCC one and it will work as long as you don't have any high frequency track cleaners or lighting installed.

DCC needs programming.
Programming is a bad choice of word. As a minimum all you need to do is set the decoder's number in each locomotive. This is usually a matter of a few key presses. That's it. You don't need to know, adjust or program anything else. Setting a video recorder is harder.

DCC isn't needed on a small layout.
DCC is ideally suited to small layouts. The ability to stop a locomotive anywhere, regardless of dead sections, is a boon to operators of compact layouts. If you had a small layout depicting a motive power depot you could park locomotives nose to tail in prototypical fashion. You could also operate the points and signals from your handheld controller rather than a control panel.

DCC isn't needed on a large layout.
DCC is ideally suited to large layouts too. The ability to select any locomotive and then run it without having to worry about setting section switches, reverse loops and isolating sections means that you can concentrate on driving the train.

You need to buy a special tester.
Like most technological gadgets offered to consumers DCC items work when you take them out of the box. In the unlikely event that they don't – take them back to the retailer.

You need a computer to get the best out of DCC.
You can link DCC up to a computer if you wish. The computer can work some, or all, of your layout if you do, but you don't have to.

It's confusing.
That's what this book is for. The ideas behind DCC are simple and you don't need to know exactly how it works in order to use it, just like you don't need to know how an internal combustion engine works in order to drive a car.

Different manufacturers' systems are not compatible.
The whole point of DCC is that any command station can control any decoder.

Where a decoder or command station offers more features than the other, you won't be able to use these extra features, but basics like speed and direction are always available however sophisticated or simple your DCC system. Add-ons to command stations, such as extra controllers or computer interfaces are not covered by the DCC standards and so can be specific to one manufacturer. There are some standards that have been adopted by other manufacturers so, for example, Lenz, ZTC and Bachmann controllers can work together.

So where did DCC come from?

Well, the idea has been around since the 1940s but it was only in the 1970s that 'multiple train control' systems started to become commercially feasible. There were a number of false starts and equipment from competing manufacturers was not compatible, meaning that once you selected one of these expensive systems you were limited to what that manufacturer offered. The early systems were not very reliable and there was limited take-up so they disappeared from the general market. However, the idea lived on. The National Model Railroad Association (NMRA) in America adopted a proposal for a set of standards for multiple train control from Lenz in Germany. They believed that if all the equipment was compatible it would benefit both manufacturers and modellers. The standards were developed; the system named DCC and made freely available for manufacturers to use. Now there are a wide range of manufacturers offering all sorts of DCC equipment. You can even buy DCC train sets from Bachmann and Hornby in the UK.

Whilst you don't need to know how DCC works in order to use it, many people are curious. If you really don't want to know how it works its magic, feel free to skip on to the next chapter.

With a conventional control system:

- You operate a controller that varies the voltage fed to the track that is connected to it.
- A locomotive on the track picks up this voltage and uses it to run the motor.
- The more voltage that is fed to the track, the faster the motor goes.
- If two locomotives are on the track that is connected to the controller then they will both move when the controller is turned on. To move them independently they each need to be on separate sections of track operated by separate controllers. To stop one of them moving it needs to be in an isolated section.

With DCC:

- You operate a controller that can select which locomotive it will operate.
- The settings on the controller are sent to a booster unit which mixes the control signal with a constant AC voltage and sends it to the track.
- The decoder in the locomotive that has been selected picks up the signal and sets its motor accordingly.
- The voltage on the track does not vary regardless of the speed or direction of any locomotive.
- If more than one locomotive is on the track then only the locomotive that has been selected will respond to the control.
- You can use one controller to control two or more locomotives; for example, you can set a train to lap a main line circuit whilst you shunt in the goods yard.

The constant voltage on the track can have a number of benefits:

- It is easy to provide constant intensity lighting for carriages.
- Many locomotive decoders come with lighting outputs to provide constant, controllable lighting.

There are fewer problems with poor electrical pick-up when running slowly. The track stays clean for longer. With conventional control systems when you are running trains each rail has an electrical charge which attracts dirt. With DCC the rails have no overall charge and so don't attract dirt.

With all the track powered all the time there are fewer chances of problems caused by faulty or incorrectly operated switches.

If you modify your layout you don't need to rewire your control panel or put in lots of extra wires.

Whilst it is more of a challenge to find space for a DCC decoder in an N gauge locomotive, it is still within the capacity of most modellers. The flexibility of DCC combined with the size benefits of N make modelling stretches of mainline railway an achievable goal. This model shows how N gauge is admirably suited to this sort of project.

Busy mainline stations are easier to operate with DCC as operators can concentrate on driving their train rather than flicking switches for tack power.
This model of Stafford station as it was in the steam days is on display at the Telford & Horsehay Steam Railway.

CHAPTER

Converting to DCC

There are many ways that you can move from conventional DC operation to DCC; which you choose will be dependent on a number of factors such as the size of your layout, number of locomotives to be converted and your budget.

It is quite possible to fit decoders to your locomotives and still operate them on conventional DC. This approach would allow you to build up a selection of DCC fitted locomotives before changing the controller(s) over. Similarly it is possible to operate locomotives without decoders on a DCC system. Neither method gives you the full functionality of a fully DCC system, but as an interim measure whilst the conversion is under way they can help to keep things operational for those times when you want to run trains.

I would not recommend converting one controller on a layout to a DCC command station and leaving the others as ordinary analogue controllers. Whilst some people suggest this as one way to convert a layout to DCC in stages, it suffers from a number of potential pitfalls. Firstly if a locomotive bridges the gap between DCC and DC controlled sections then the AC track voltage can cause damage to electronic components in transistorised controllers. Similarly the DC voltage can cause unexpected results in the DCC controlled area. Secondly the widespread use of common return on analogue circuits can lead to the AC and DC voltages appearing in places where they ought not to be. Finally systems that superimpose a high frequency AC voltage on the analogue DC voltage, such as constant coach lighting systems and high-frequency track cleaners, like those produced by Relco, will disrupt, and quite possibly damage, the DCC system.

Converting The Controller First

This is only really viable on a layout with a single controller. The different architecture of DCC and analogue systems makes it difficult to directly replace a multiple controller analogue system with an equivalent DCC system unless the locomotives are already equipped with DCC decoders.

Assuming that you are using a single controller, all you need to do is to replace the existing analogue controller with a DCC unit and select the analogue loco channel. All the section switches will work as before. Of course you will still need to use the section switches to isolate your DC locomotives.

BELOW: A typical multi-controller system with section switches to connect the controllers to different sections of the layout.

BELOW: DCC locomotive decoders can replace analogue controllers to give control of the layout. This system cannot be used on layouts wired for common return.

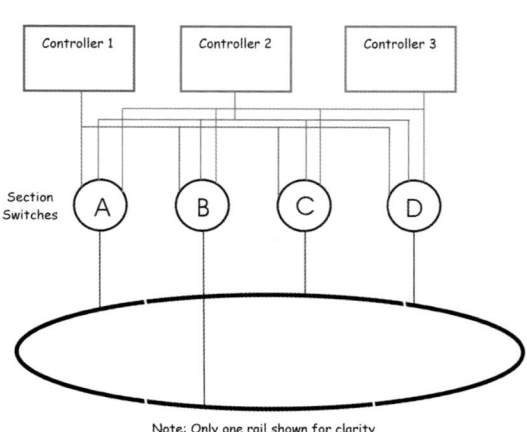

For those of you who use more than one controller and are determined to convert the controllers first, the only viable solution is to replace them with a DCC unit with the requisite number of additional controllers. The DCC output is connected not to the track, but a power bus which feeds a number of locomotive decoders which replace the old analogue controllers. Unfortunately this system does not work with common return wiring so unless your electrical sections are already isolated on both rails this will involve more wiring, work and materials – probably more than converting straight to DCC.

Converting The Locomotives First

Advantage:
All locomotives can be operated during the locomotive conversion process. No changes are needed to controls or wiring until the DCC command station is installed.

Disadvantage:
You don't get the benefits of DCC operation until the locomotives have all been converted.

Most DCC decoders have the ability to operate on analogue DC layouts. This enables you to fit decoders to your locomotives as time and funds allow before switching over to DCC. You will probably want to set up a small DCC test track with a command station so that you can test the decoder installation in each locomotive, set the decoder parameters and get used to operating the system. Meanwhile your layout will continue to work just the way that it did before.

There are a small number of possible pitfalls to watch out for:

Most decoders have an analogue (DC) mode that enables them to be operated on a DC layout.

- The analogue (DC) mode can be disabled on any decoder. This setting is found in CV 29 (see Chapter 8 Configuring Locomotive Decoders for more details). If the locomotive is happy on the DCC test track but will not respond on the layout then you need to turn the analogue mode on, or check that the decoder supports analogue (DC) operation.

- Ensure that there is a brief spell of zero voltage on the track when you change direction on the controller. If your controller does not do this then it is quite possible that decoder equipped locomotives will not recognise the change of direction and either continue travelling in the same direction or stop dead. The easiest way to establish if this is a problem is to try it and see. Get a decoder equipped locomotive up to about half speed and flick the direction switch. If the locomotive changes direction (hopefully by slowing down to a stop first and then accelerating again) all is well. Otherwise you will need to add a separate direction switch on the output of the controller. This should be a Double Pole Double Throw Centre-Off Switch with Break Before Make contacts. The switch should be wired as shown in the diagram below and used

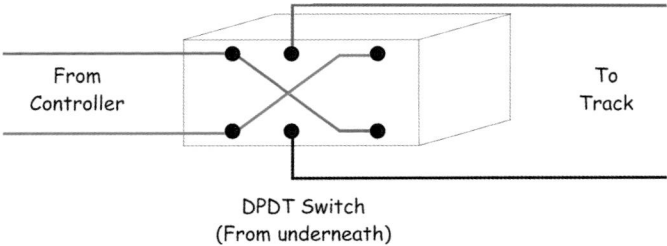

From Controller

To Track

DPDT Switch
(From underneath)

How to wire a reversing switch between the controller and the track.

INSTEAD of the one on the controller. Placing some tape over the controller's switch will stop it being used by accident. These switches are available from most electronic component suppliers. Purchasing a switch with a centre-off position allows you to disconnect the controller totally from the track and ensures that you must go through a zero voltage state when changing direction. Three suggested suppliers are listed below.

Maplin Electronics Ltd.	*part no.*	*JK30H 10A Toggle DPDT F*
Rapid Electronics Ltd.	*part no.*	*75-0145 DPDT Centre-off*
Squires Model & Craft Tools	*part no.*	*STT200 Standard Toggle DPDT C/Off On-Off-On*

- If your analogue controllers produce pulsed power (for example, half-wave rectification, pulse width modulation) then decoder equipped locomotives can sometimes run erratically. To solve this you will need to connect two capacitors across the output of each analogue controller as shown in the diagram below. These capacitors are available from most electronic component suppliers. Three suggested suppliers are listed below.

How to convert pulsed power DC for use when running DCC decoder fitted locomotives from an analogue (DC) controller. The capacitors smooth the pulsed output providing a constant DC voltage.

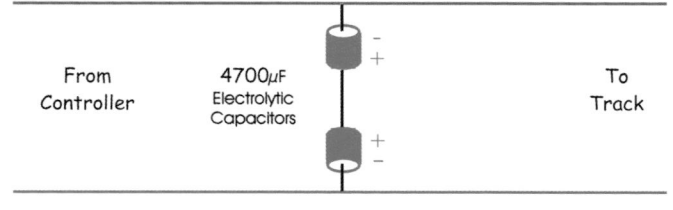

Maplin Electronics Ltd.	*part no.*	*AT24B AxlElect 4700µF 35V*
Rapid Electronics Ltd.	*part no.*	*11-1418 4700µF 35V radial electrolytic capacitor*
Squires Model & Craft Tools	*part no.*	*541-193 35V 4700µF capacitor*

The Next Step

As well as fitting decoders to your locomotives you should also consider working on the layout wiring ready for the changeover. Identify any extra track feeds or section gaps that will be needed and install them ready for use. Ideally every piece of rail should be connected to a wire; do not rely on fishplates for electrical connections.

Reversing loops, turntables and wyes will also need to be considered. Just as with analogue control there are various ways to arrange these on a DCC system (see Chapter 6 Wiring for DCC).

Once you are ready to turn on the DCC system you will need to disconnect the old analogue controllers and section switches. The tracks should be connected to the track bus (see Chapter 6 Wiring for DCC) and the DCC controllers connected up. Finally, remove the locomotives that don't have decoders fitted from the track and switch on.

Something To Avoid

Depending on your layout you might be tempted to try to combine analogue and DCC controllers, for example using DCC on the branch line and the existing analogue controllers on the main line. Whilst it is technically possible to do this it does run the risk of damaging both control systems as well as the locomotives.

Firstly the analogue and DCC sections of the layout need to be completely electrically isolated. You cannot get the systems to work together if you have used common return wiring. More importantly when a locomotive bridges the gap between the two sections the DCC track voltage can flow into the analogue section of the layout. This can cause a voltage difference of over 20V to appear on the track. Many motors and analogue controllers will not take kindly to this kind of abuse.

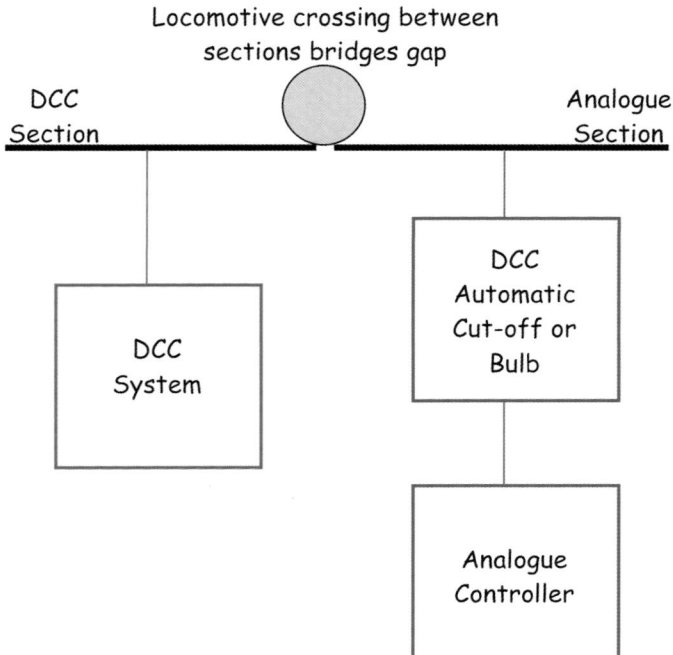

You need to protect your analogue controllers if you have both DCC and analogue controlled sections on the same layout.

It is possible to buy, or build, devices that detect the DCC voltage and cut off the supply to the analogue controller. This protects both the controller and the locomotives. An alternative is to use a large bulb, typically a car tail light or similar, rated at 12V 5W or more. This will illuminate when the DCC voltage is present and provide a measure of protection. Even so, special wiring will be needed at any point where trains can cross from one control system to the other. Typically this would involve a length of track, electrically isolated at both ends, that can be fed by either control system via a changeover switch. The train would be driven into the section by one controller and stopped. The switch would then be thrown and the train driven out by the other controller.

CHAPTER

3

Command Stations, Boosters and Cabs

RIGHT: *The DCS 100 is the combined command station and booster supplied as part of the Digitrax Super Chief set.*

BELOW: *This Lenz LH30 hand-held controller is an example of a simple cab that can be used to control a DCC system.*

The control side of DCC systems consists of three building blocks. Depending on the system that you buy, one or more of them may be in the same box.

The cab is the item that allows you to control the speed and direction of one or more locomotives. Some cabs use knobs, some have buttons and those manufactured by NCE have both! Depending on the system, the cab may also be able to control a number of locomotive functions, such as lights and sound, change points and set locomotive decoder settings. A layout may have a number of cabs so that a number of people can run trains at the same time.

The command station is the brains of the system. It takes information from the cabs and converts it into DCC format. A layout needs only one command station. If you try to install more than one then they will send conflicting DCC signals along the track and nothing will work.

The booster is the brawn to the command station's brains. It takes the weak DCC signal and amplifies it so that it is powerful enough to power locomotives and accessories. Large layouts and those where a large number of locomotives or accessories will be in use will need a number of boosters in order to provide sufficient power.

There are DCC systems to suit most requirements from a child's train set through to a complex multi-operator empire. Selecting a suitable system is a matter of matching the facilities offered to your requirements and budget. Whilst you can operate any DCC decoder with any DCC command station the cabs, command stations and boosters are not necessarily compatible between manufacturers.

By and large the more flexibility and functionality that you require from your DCC system, the more that you will have to

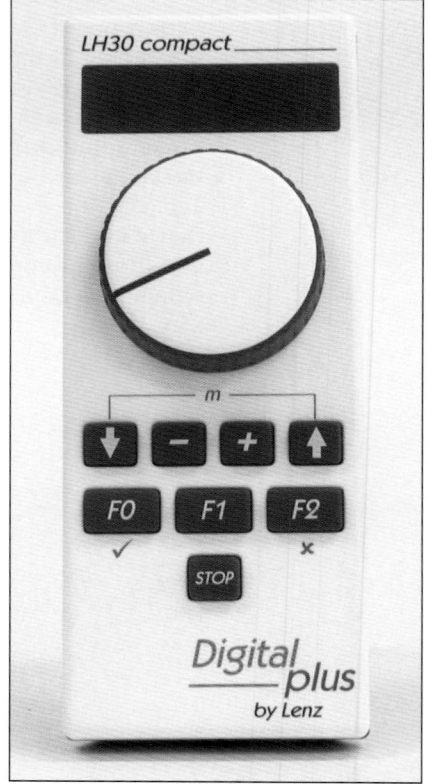

pay. Fortunately in many cases it is possible to add extra units to a basic system to expand it without having to discard your original items.

At the bottom end of the range of price and functionality are the simple systems, such as the Bachmann E-Z Command, which have limited capability but are exceedingly simple to install and operate. At the top end of the range are systems which allow more cabs and boosters than you are likely to ever need, can be interfaced to a computer as well as operating many functions and accessories. In between these extremes are some mid-range systems that have sufficient functionality and flexibility for most British layouts.

Many of the DCC manufacturers and retailers have displays at the major model railway exhibitions and if you are considering an expensive system then you would be well advised to go along and try it for yourself. However good a system appears on paper there are a number of questions that can be answered only when you see the system in reality.

- If it is a walkaround, does the cab fit comfortably in your hand?
- Is the speed control easy to operate?
- Are the buttons large enough for you to operate comfortably?
- Can you read the display?

I have included a table of most of the DCC starter sets available on the UK market at the time of writing (2006). Bear in mind that the DCC market changes rapidly and new units appear, features are added and updated on a regular basis so please use it only as a guide rather than the final arbiter in your decision.

The key questions that you need to ask yourself are as follows:

How many locomotives am I likely to have?
If you have room for only eight locomotives on your layout then even if you own eighty you can get by with a system that has nine locomotive addresses. If you are installing DCC on a club layout with a vast pool of locomotives then you may need the ability to use over 1,000 addresses.

How many locomotives will be running at once?
The more locomotives that are running at once, the more power you need. Don't forget that with DCC you can operate several locomotives at once. For example, you could have two trains looping the main line, one double-headed, whilst you shunt the yard. That would be four locomotives just on one cab.

DCC enables you not only to run any locomotive, anywhere on your layout, but also to park it anywhere. This is a great benefit if your layout includes a motive power depot.
Picture: Kier Hardy
www.kierhardy.co.uk

Will I be using carriage lighting?

The constant voltage on the track makes it easy to install things like carriage lighting – but all those lights take current. This needs to be added on to your power requirement.

How many cabs do I need?

Each operator will need their own cab. You may also want some extras to save switching between different locomotives in use at the same time.

Do I want walkaround control?

Many DCC systems have both fixed and walkaround cabs available. In the past most UK layouts have used fixed control systems where the operator sits in one location with all the necessary controls to hand.

With walkaround cabs the operators can move around with their trains. Obviously this means that any controls must be situated near to where they are used but as DCC removes the need for block and power switches you only need to consider controls for points, signals and other accessories. If you use DCC to control these items as well then everything can be operated from the walkaround cab. It is, of course, possible to have a combination of fixed and

The ZTC 521 is a typical walkaround controller. It includes a selection of buttons, a speed control and a small display.
Picture: ZTC Controls Limited

walkaround cabs if you wish.

Walkaround cabs come in two varieties: tethered and remote control. Tethered cabs are connected to the layout by a long cable. You plug these into sockets placed around the layout. You can unplug the cab and move it to a different socket without having to stop the train. Remote control cabs use radio or infra-red signals to link to a receiver situated under the layout. These are more expensive and less common than the tethered variety.

With controllers of this type there is a trade-off between number of controls and functionality. If there are a few buttons then it is easy to perform simple operations but can be difficult, or even impossible, to do more complex tasks. If there are a lot of buttons then it requires fewer key presses to do complex tasks but it is easier to get the wrong button when you are watching the train rather than looking at the controller.

Is there a cab bus?

Many DCC systems have a system that allows extra cabs, boosters and other accessories to be connected together easily. This is normally called a cab, or control, bus. Where a common standard is used equipment such as cabs from different manufacturers can be used together.

Two common cab buses are the Lenz XpressNet (also called X Bus III) and the Digitrax LocoNet. The two systems are not compatible with each other but any XpressNet compatible item can be plugged in to, and used with, an XpressNet bus regardless of the manufacturer. Similarly any LocoNet compatible item can be used on a LocoNet bus. If the manufacturer of your chosen DCC system has their own type of cab bus then you will be restricted to using only their cabs, boosters and accessories.

Do I want to operate points and signals?

You can use DCC to run locomotives but stick to conventional systems to operate points and signals, or you can use DCC for those too. You can even use DCC for the points and conventional control for the locomotives if you wish, probably as an interim measure whilst you fit your locomotives with decoders.

With DCC you have the option of controlling points and signals as well as locomotives.
Picture: Kier Hardy
www.kierhardy.co.uk

Do I want a computer interface?

A computer can drive trains whilst you act as signalman, can be the signalman whilst you drive trains or can drive trains at the same time that you do, providing other traffic for you to work around.

Do I have any special track formations?

Wyes, reversing loops and turntables all need special treatment. Do you want to operate the voltage changeover manually or automatically?

How many functions do I need on my locomotives?

Modern light systems can take up four decoder outputs. Then there is sound, remote uncoupling, smoke generators . . .

Can I install it all at once or do I want to do it in stages?

Features like a computer interface or automatically operated reversing loops can be added later. Point and signal operation could be converted to DCC once the locomotive conversion is complete.

How much can I afford?

Be realistic. It is easy to get carried away with features that you may never need or use.

Starter Set Comparison

Unit	Bachmann E-Z Command	Hornby Select	Hornby Elite	MRC/Gaugemaster Prodigy Advance
Speed control	Knob	Knob	Knob (two throttles in one case)	Knob
Maximum number of extra controllers	At least 2			Up to 99
Maximum number of locomotive addresses	9	60	255	9999
Speed steps	128	14, 28 or 128	14, 28 or 128	14, 28 or 128
Maximum current	1A	1A (4A option)	4A	3.5A
Additional power stations	Yes	No	No	No
Accessory control (points etc.)	No	Yes (40 items)	Yes	Yes
Route control	No	No	No	Up to 31 routes each operating up to 8 accessories
Consists	No	–	–	Advanced
Other expansion	Lenz X Bus	XpressNet	Lenz XpressNet & USB port	MRC Throttle Bus
Reversing loop capability	Extra module available			Extra module available
Number of functions	9 (F0 – F8)	8 (F0 – F7)	8 (F0 – F7)	20
Programming capability	Decoder address only	Yes	Yes	Yes
Programming on the main	All other locomotives must be removed from layout	No	–	Yes
Walkaround controller	No	Yes	No	Yes
Decoders included	No	No	No	No
Analogue locomotive operation	Yes	Yes	Yes	No
Guide price	£45.95	£70.00	£140.00	£225.00
Power supply	Included	Included	Included	Included

The Bachmann E-Z Command controller is a basic system that lacks functionality to program CVs or accommodate more than ten locomotives on your layout.

Unit	Lenz Digital Plus Compact Set	Lenz Start Set 90	Lenz Start Set 100	NCE Powerhouse Pro 5	NCE PowerCab
Speed control	Knob	Knob	Button	Buttons and thumb wheel	Buttons and thumb wheel
Maximum number of extra controllers	5	31	31	62	62
Maximum number of locomotive addresses	99	9999	9999	9999	9999
Speed steps	14, 28, 128	14, 27, 28, 128	14, 27, 28, 128	14, 28, 128	14, 28, 128
Maximum current	2.5A	5A	5A	5A	1.7A
Additional power stations	Yes – maximum of 3	Yes	Yes	Yes	Yes
Accessory control (points etc.)	Yes – 100 items	Yes – 1000 items	Yes – 1024 items	Yes – 2044 items	Yes – 2044 items
Route control	No	No	No	Yes – 256 routes with up to 10 items per route	Yes – 16 routes with up to 8 items per route
Consists	Advanced	Universal/Advanced	Universal/Advanced	Universal/Advanced	Universal/Advanced
Other expansion	Lenz XpressNet	Lenz XpressNet	Lenz XpressNet	Built-in computer interface (RS-232)	Optional computer interface
Reversing loop capability available	Extra module available	Extra module available	Extra module available	Extra module available	Extra module available
Number of functions	3 (F0 – F2)	13 (F0 – F12)	13 (F0 – F12)	13 (F0 – F12)	13 (F0 – F12)
Programming capability	Yes	Yes	Yes	Yes	Yes
Programming on the main	No	Yes	Yes	Yes	Yes
Walkaround controller	No	Yes	Yes	Yes	Yes
Decoders included	2 loco & 1 accessory	No	No	No	No
Analogue locomotive operation	Yes	Yes	Yes	No	No
Guide price	£175.00	£199.90	£244.50	£275.00	£95.00
Power Supply	Included	TR100UK – £36	TR100UK – £36	Included	Included

Unit	ZTC 2050 Fireman's Set	ZTC2003 Footplate Set
Speed control	Thumb wheel	Regulator handle
Maximum number of extra controllers	30	3
Maximum number of locomotive addresses	9999	9999
Speed steps	14, 28, 128	14, 28, 128
Maximum current	4A	5A
Additional power stations	Yes	Yes
Accessory control (points etc.)	Yes – 4000 items	Yes – 4043 items
Route control	Yes – 10 routes (upgrade available)	Yes – 16 routes (upgrade available)
Consists	Yes – UK practice	Yes – UK practice
Other expansion	X Bus III	X Bus III
Reversing loop capability	Extra module available	Extra module available
Number of functions	6 (F0 – F5)	9 (F0 – F8)
Programming capability	Yes	Yes
Programming on the main	No	No
Walkaround controller	No	No
Decoders included	1 loco	2 loco & 1 accessory
Analogue locomotive operation	Yes	Yes
Guide price	£199.95	£575.00
Power supply	Included	Included

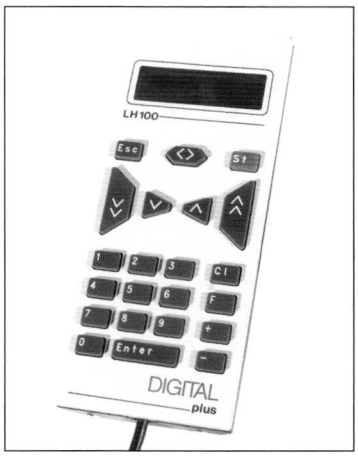

The Lenz LH 100 cab offers a wide range of functions in a compact unit. It is quite capable of operating an extensive layout from the palm of your hand.

The ZTC 511 controller was specifically designed for the UK.
Picture: ZTC Controls Limited

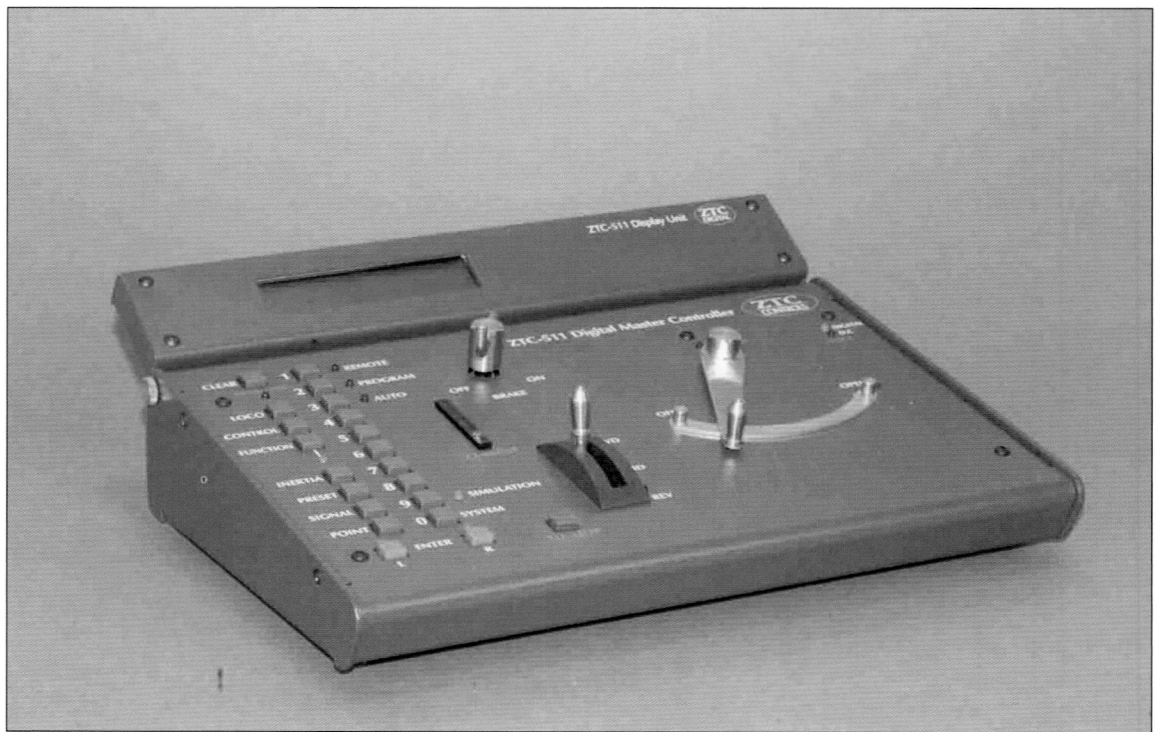

Unit	Digitrax Zephyr	Digitrax Super Empire Builder	Digitrax Super Chief	Roco
Speed control	Regulator lever	Knob (two throttles in one case)	Knob (two throttles in one case)	Knob
Maximum number of extra controllers	10	21	119	4
Maximum number of locomotive addresses	9000	9000	9000	99
Speed steps	14, 28, 128	128	128	14, 28, 128
Maximum current	2.5A	5A	5A (8A available)	2.7A
Additional power stations	Yes	Yes	Yes	Yes – up to 4
Accessory control (points, etc.)	999	999	999	Extra unit available
Route control	No	No	Yes – 32 routes of up to 8 items	Extra unit available
Consists	No	Universal/Advanced	Universal/Advanced	–
Other expansion	LocoNet	LocoNet	LocoNet	XpressNet
Reversing loop capability	Extra module available	Extra module available	Extra module available	Extra module available
Number of functions	9 (F0 – F8)	13 (F0 – F12)	13 (F0 – F12)	5
Programming capability	Yes	Yes	Yes	Yes
Programming on the main	Yes	Yes	Yes	No
Walkaround controller	No	Yes	Yes	Yes
Decoders included	No	No	No	Set includes DCC German outline locomotive
Analogue locomotive operation	Yes	Yes	Yes	No
Guide price	£145.00	£220.00	£285.00	£95.00
Power supply	Included	Included	Included	Included

Unit	Roco 10792 Loco Mouse R3	Roco 10810 Multi Mouse	Bachmann Dynamis
Speed control	Knob	Knob	Joystick
Maximum number of extra controllers	14	–	–
Maximum number of locomotive addresses	99	9999	9999
Speed steps	14, 28, 128	128	–
Maximum current	–	–	–
Additional power stations	–	–	Yes
Accessory control (points, etc.)	No	Yes – up to 24	–
Route control	No	No	–
Consists	–	–	Yes
Other expansion	–	XpressNet	XpressNet
Reversing loop capability	Extra module available	Extra module available	Extra module available
Number of functions	5 (F0 – F4)	21 (F0 – F20)	21 (F0 – F20)
Programming capability	Yes	Yes	Yes
Programming on the main	–	–	–
Walkaround controller	Yes	Yes	Yes (wireless)
Decoders included	No	No	No
Guide price	£65.55	£75.55	£90.00
Power supply	Included	Included	Included

Real locomotives are often parked buffer to buffer, no matter how much spare siding space is available. This is easy to replicate anywhere on the layout when you use DCC. With analogue DC you are limited by the location of isolating sections, each of which needs its own switch and wiring. This photo shows Nos D2902 and 42366 at Bletchley in 1961.
Picture: Author's collection

Locomotive Decoders

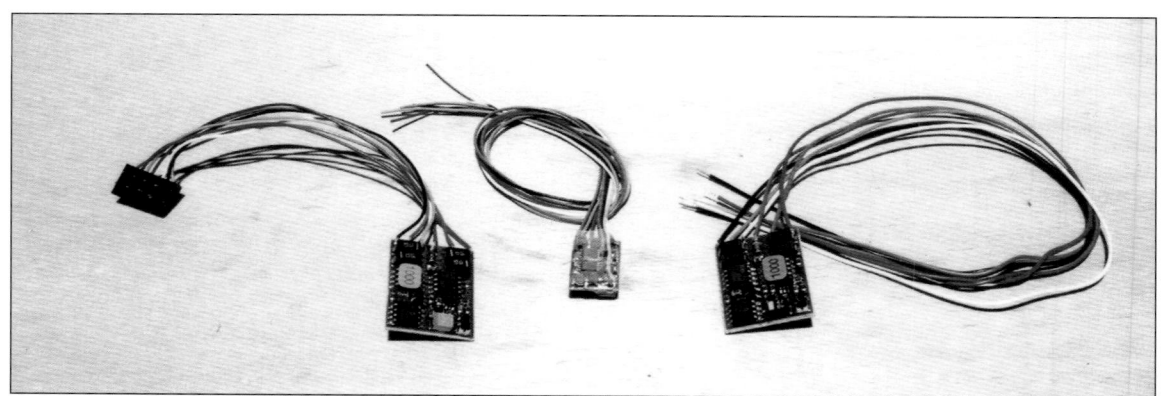

Decoders come in a wide variety of shapes and sizes and with an array of features. All of these have a bearing on their suitability for use in a specific locomotive. Fortunately you can use any suitable decoder regardless of which type of command station you have. You may not be able to use all the command station features, or all the decoder features, but the basics will be compatible across the products of all suppliers.

As an example, if you have a command station that can operate only five functions you can still fit decoders with nine functions to your locomotives – it is just that four of the functions will never be used unless you upgrade the command station. Similarly if the command station can control more functions than the decoder then the extra functions will be ignored. The basics of speed, direction and address will be controllable regardless of how well matched the decoder and command station specifications are.

Before you even think about what type of decoder to fit in a locomotive you should ensure that it performs well on a standard DC power pack. DCC is not a magic cure for a bad motor or mechanism that is clogged with fluff. You will need to remove the model's body anyway, so for models that have already clocked up a few miles it is a good opportunity to give the mechanism a thorough clean and to lubricate the gear trains. For a brand new model it is imperative to test it on DC so that you are happy with it before you start doing anything that might invalidate the guarantee.

When you start to look at decoders you will quickly realise that there are a wide range of seemingly similar items and choosing between them can seem to be a problem. So what are the factors that govern the choice of decoder for a specific locomotive?

Locomotive decoders come in a range of shapes, sizes and specifications.

Current rating

The electric motor in your locomotive draws its power from the decoder. The current rating, measured in amps (for example 3A is 3 amps) is a measure of the power that the decoder can deliver continuously without being damaged. Bigger models with bigger motors draw more current than smaller ones and, in general, modern motors draw less current than old ones.

As a rule of thumb most Z or N gauge models draw 0.75A or less. Modern OO or HO models typically draw less than 1A, with older ones needing up to 1.5A. O gauge and larger models can draw as much as 4A. Don't forget to allow for lighting and any other electrically powered features that may be installed in the locomotive when deciding how powerful a decoder you need.

You will often read that it is necessary to know, or determine, the stall current of a locomotive before you fit a decoder. To establish the stall current you will need to connect a meter between a conventional DC power pack and the track and set it to a suitable amp scale then hold the locomotive so that the wheels cannot rotate and give it a burst of full power. This is a fairly risky process as you may damage the model or its motor. In truth there is no need to measure the stall current precisely as decoders come with a limited range of current capacities. For an electric locomotive to be drawing the stall current it would need to have something wedged in the gears or wheels in order to bring it to a complete halt. Even the worst derailment will normally leave the wheels free to rotate so a complete stop is a fairly unlikely eventuality. It is far more important that your chosen decoder can provide the current needed for normal continuous running. By and large, models built in the past few years have a lower current consumption than those built years ago.

It is not possible for manufacturers or reviewers to quote accurate current consumption figures as these will vary not only for different locomotives of the same type, but for the same locomotive at different times, depending on the wear, lubrication and cleanliness of the mechanism.

Coreless Motors – A Warning

High quality coreless motors, such as those produced by Escap, need special consideration. Due to their design they are unsuited to the pulsed DC provided by standard DCC locomotive decoders. This causes them to heat up rapidly and can cause them to burn out very quickly. This type of motor needs pure DC, or something close to it.

If you have locomotives fitted with coreless motors then you need to install high quality decoders with 'silent' or 'high frequency' drive and, ideally, adjustable-back EMF. Suitable decoders include the ESU LokPilot, Lenz Gold series and Zimo range.

Also you should NEVER run a locomotive fitted with a coreless motor as an analogue locomotive on a DCC system. Again the pulsed DC power will cause the motor to heat up and burn out.

How do you know if you've got coreless motors? If you need to ask then you probably haven't. They are expensive motors normally only fitted to kit builds or conversions.

Size

Obvious really, but it is easy to overestimate the space that you have available when the locomotive's body is in place. Check the dimensions of the decoder that you intend to use, and if you don't have one make a mock-up from cardboard, then see if it will fit. Don't forget that you will need space for the wires as well.

In some models finding space can be a big problem and it may be necessary to cut away parts of weights or the chassis. Don't forget useful hidey holes such as the fuel tanks underneath diesel locomotives and steam engine cabs and tenders.

Connection

Some models are now supplied 'DCC ready' and come with a standard socket that a decoder can be plugged into. If you have such a model then you need a decoder with a plug. Other models need one which ends in wires. You can, of course, always convert a plug fitted decoder to a wire connection one by cutting the plug off – but as you will probably have paid extra for it in the first place you won't want to make a habit of it.

The Bachmann website (www.bachmann.co.uk) includes a listing of the locomotives currently in their range that are fitted with a DCC socket. The socket blanking plug is also illustrated on the exploded diagram included with each locomotive, so you don't need to take the body off to establish if a socket is fitted. All Heljan locomotives are fitted with a DCC socket. For Hornby locomotives you can download service sheets from the Hornby website (www.hornby.co.uk) which include an exploded diagram showing the DCC blanking plug, part number X9255, on locos fitted with a DCC socket.

Most decoders that have a plug fitted come with an NMRA 8 pin plug that matches the socket in most 'DCC ready' locomotives. Large scale models, and the corresponding decoders, come with a 4 pin version designed for carrying higher currents whilst there is also a rarer 6 pin version intended for N scale.

Recently 21 pin sockets have appeared on some models, including some from Bachmann. These are not yet standard and special converters are needed to use them with eight pin plug fitted sockets.

Some manufacturers mark pin number 1 on the socket, usually with a small triangle. If you can't work out which is pin 1 – don't worry, the connections have been specified so that it will not harm the locomotive or decoder if you plug it in the wrong way round. If you do plug the decoder in incorrectly the locomotive may run but the lights won't work. Just unplug the decoder and plug it in the other way around.

Standard DCC plug/socket wiring (2 rows of 4 pins)

Pin	Wire Colour	Function
1	Orange	Motor +ve
2	Yellow	Rear light (F2)
3	Green	F3
4	Black	Track pick up (left rail)
5	Grey	Motor –ve
6	White	Front light (F1)
7	Blue	Light/function common
8	Red	Track pick-up (right rail)

Large scale DCC plug/socket wiring (2 rows of 2 pins)

Pin	Wire Colour	Function
1	Grey	Motor –ve
2	Orange	Motor +ve
3	Black	Track pick-up (left rail)
4	Red	Track pick-up (right rail)

Small DCC plug/socket wiring (1 row of 6 pins)

Pin	Wire Colour	Function
1	Orange	Motor +ve
2	Grey	Motor –ve
3	Red	Track pick-up (right rail)
4	Black	Track pick-up (left rail)
5	White	Front light (F1)
6	Yellow	Rear light (F2)

If you are installing a DCC decoder with wires rather than a plug then the diagram on page 25 shows how the decoder is connected between the track pick-ups and the motor. The red decoder wire goes to the right rail (looking forwards) and the black one to the left rail. The orange wire goes to the motor terminal that was connected to the right rail, and the grey wire to the other motor terminal. If you get the red and black swapped around, or the grey and orange, all that will happen is that the locomotive will go backwards instead of forwards. However, you must be careful not to mix up red and orange or grey and black as this will damage your decoder.

Functions

The function outputs can do all sorts of things – provided that the model is equipped to use them. Lighting is a favourite feature and to correctly replicate modern UK practice you need four function outputs. Other features that are suitable for function control include horns or whistles, remote control uncoupling and smoke generators.

Whilst some new locomotives produced for the UK market now include factory fitted lights, many still do not. If you wish to install lighting Express

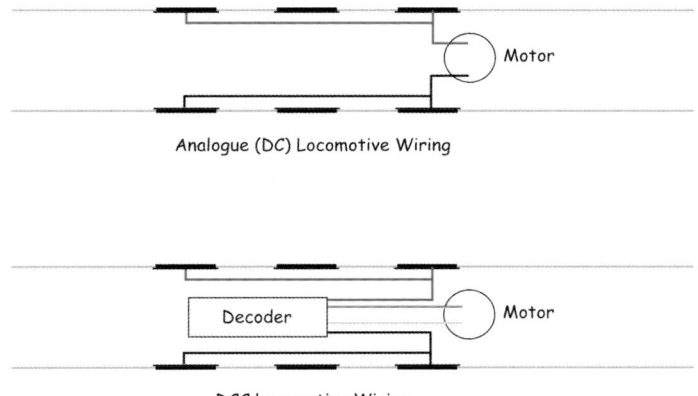

Analogue (DC) Locomotive Wiring

DCC Locomotive Wiring

Fitting a DCC decoder to a locomotive involves rerouting the power picked up from the track through the decoder rather than straight to the motor.

Lighting with LEDs

Light Emitting Diodes (LEDs) have many advantages over the traditional light bulb when it comes to lighting on model locomotives. They are available in a range of small sizes, they generate no heat and have a virtually unlimited life if treated properly. In addition they draw less current than light bulbs and so you can run a number of LEDs from a decoder function output without overloading it.

It is important to limit the current and voltage that flows through the LED to avoid damaging it. It is also necessary to connect it the right way round. The anode should be connected to the more positive side of the circuit and the cathode to the more negative side.

On a locomotive decoder the blue wire is the common positive. All the LED anodes, for all the functions, should be connected to this wire via a resistor.

The LED's cathode is connected to the appropriate function wire: white for F1 (normally headlights), yellow for F2 (normally tail lights), green for F3 and purple for F4.

To turn the LEDs on or off all you need to do is select the appropriate function on the cab. It doesn't matter if the locomotive is moving or not – the lights will stay on (or off) and not dim or brighten.

You can run more than one LED from each function output. For example, you might wish to run two headlights and one tail light. The circuit would look like this:

The Resistor
On a locomotive decoder the blue wire is the common positive. All the LED anodes, for all the functions, should be connected to this wire via a resistor. Typically this should be a 680R 0.5W. If you want the lights to be dimmer use a higher value resistor such as 820R or 1K. If you want the lights to be brighter (especially if you are using a lower track voltage) then a lower value resistor such as 560R or 470R should be used. Each LED needs to run through its own resistor.

The LED
LEDs are available in a range of colours and sizes. For 4mm scale models the most useful size is probably 3mm which is ideal for many locomotive headlights. Red LEDs can be used for tail lights; white LEDs come in two varieties: blue-white which are ideal for the high-intensity lights used on modern rolling stock and yellow-white which look more like a traditional headlight.

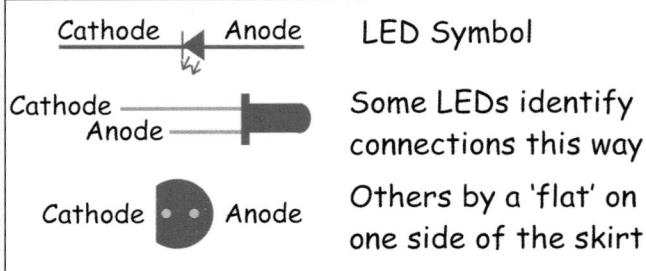

It is important to connect the LED the right way round. If it is connected the wrong way round the LED will not light and if it is subjected to more than about 5V when connected the wrong way round it will never work again. If you are in any doubt as to which lead is which, test the LED out on a couple of 1.5V batteries or the function output of a decoder – but if you do this, don't forget the resistor.

LEFT: Operating a number of LEDS from one function

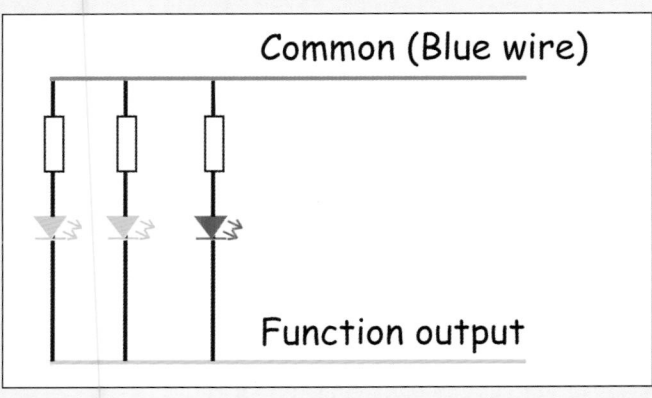

Common (Blue wire)

Function output

Models supply kits for many diesel classes and oil type head and tail lamps for steam outline models.

Sound

The range of sounds available for UK models is increasing slowly. Whilst sound equipped decoders are expensive they are very impressive, especially as the sound is automatically matched to the motion of the model.

One problem with sound equipped decoders is finding room for the larger sized decoder and accompanying speaker. In 4mm scale diesel locomotives the between bogies fuel tank is one possible place for hiding the speaker. As technology advances these units are becoming smaller and it is now possible to obtain decoders and speakers to fit into N scale locomotives. Another problem is that the range of UK locomotive sounds available is limited at the moment, but it is expanding all the time.

When installing a sound equipped decoder you should always try to fit the largest speaker that the locomotive can accommodate as this will give better sound quality and volume. In addition rectangular speakers, where available, usually have a better frequency response and are preferable to circular ones.

Never fit a sound system to a noisy locomotive as the mechanical noise will drown out that expensive sound. Similarly you should not fit sound systems to locomotives fitted with old open frame motors as these can often generate radio frequency interference which may be picked up by the decoder circuitry. If possible you should always try to use locomotives fitted with high quality 'can' motors for this type of installation.

If you have a small layout then you could opt to install the sound equipped decoder underneath the layout, rather than in a locomotive. It would need to be wired into the track bus and could be used in conjunction with any suitable locomotive. To operate it you would simply use the DCC consist facility that enables a number of locomotives to be operated as a set. This would mean that the decoder's sounds would reflect the locomotive's operation. Mounting the decoder under the layout would also allow the use of a much larger speaker with an improvement in sound quality. You could, of course, install a number of decoders in this way so that you could have a number of different locomotives

---

Smoke Units

Some model railway locomotives come equipped with smoke units and these must be given special attention when converting to DCC operation. Whilst there are smoke units specially manufactured for use with DCC, the ones fitted to existing locomotives will be different in that they work at a lower voltage and usually draw more current.

Whatever you do, do not leave the smoke unit connected across the pick-ups. The units are not designed to work on the 14V or more that DCC systems put on the tracks. Unless specifically designed for DCC, smoke units cannot be run directly off a decoder function output. Typically smoke units require around 150mA whilst most decoder outputs provide about 100mA.

Possible solutions are:

To connect the smoke unit across the motor terminals. This means that it will operate exactly as it used to, only smoking when the motor is operating.

To connect two function outputs together as a single feed. For example, connect the green and purple wires to one terminal and the blue wire to the other. Then set the F3 and F4 outputs to both operate from the same function key (see CV 33-46 in Chapter 8 Configuring Locomotive Decoders). This doubles the current available and should provide enough power to work the smoke unit without damaging the decoder. This enables you to turn the smoke on and off as required. You will also need to fit a suitable resistor to reduce the voltage supplied to the smoke unit.

Fit a DCC compatible smoke unit in its place and operate that from a single function output.

If you are fitting a new smoke unit you should pick one that is designed for use with DCC. The Seuthe range includes four such units, numbers 11, 12, 23 and 24. Each draws 70mA and works on supplies up to 22V. In the UK Seuthe smoke units can be purchased from Express Models and M G Sharp Models amongst others.

apparently producing sound at the same time and match the type of sound to the type of locomotive.

Sound equipped decoders for UK outline models are available from South West Digital and ZTC Controls. South West Digital provide decoders with sounds from a number of British diesel locomotive classes. ZTC Controls provide a diesel and a GWR steam sound decoder. In addition Bachmann market ready-to-run locomotives equipped with DCC decoders and sound.

One last warning: sound equipped decoders are very easily damaged so make sure that you read, and follow, the instructions supplied with them.

Special Features and Extra Functions

Some decoder ranges have special features that match their manufacturer's command stations. If you wish to use these features then you are tied to specific decoders.

One of the things that many newcomers to DCC find mystifying is the wide variation in prices for locomotive decoders. This difference is largely due to the features that are included. Some decoders support only a limited number of configuration variables (CVs) which limits their flexibility. Others may have extra power, a smaller size or more function outputs. Many of the more expensive decoders have sophisticated systems for getting the best performance out of your locomotives including feedback (back-EMF monitoring) and other techniques for different types of motor.

People keep on finding extra uses for the function outputs of decoders. Express Models supply lighting kits for modern diesel locomotives that use eight functions just for the lights. These are: (1) Forward marker lights (2) Reverse marker lights (3) Forward tail lights (4) Reverse tail lights (5) Forward white headlight (6) Reverse white headlight (7) Forward cab interior light (8) Reverse cab interior light. Add sound, operating fans, remote uncoupling, a smoke unit and you have a lot of functions.

If you need more functions than are available on a standard decoder then it is possible to install a second 'function-only' decoder, such as the Lenz LX100F in the locomotive. This type of decoder has function outputs but no motor control circuitry. You can install several function-only decoders in the same locomotive to work in combination with the locomotive decoder or install a function-only decoder by itself in a piece of rolling stock that does not need motor control, such as the trailing power car in a multiple unit set.

All decoders set to the same locomotive address

Function only decoder   Standard Decoder   Function only decoder

F1 - Headlights   Motor   F3 - Interior lights
F2 - Tail lights   F3 - Interior lights   F4 - Smoke Unit
F3 - Interior lights   F5 - Headlights
F4 - Smoke Unit   F6 - Tail lights

If you install multiple decoders in the same locomotive, you will have to make sure that you can program the decoders independently and you might have to carry out the programming before installation. If you are using decoders in different vehicles of a set, such as a multiple unit, then each decoder can be programmed individually by placing each vehicle on the programming track in turn. In both cases all the decoders should be set to the same locomotive address.

Installation

This chapter covers the installation of DCC decoders in a number of different locomotives and shows the different techniques that enable most commercial models to be converted to operate on DCC. All types of decoder are fitted in the same way so there is no need to use the same decoders as shown in the examples. In many cases I have used low-priced decoders. Many people start with these and then replace them with higher specification items as they progress and find that they want to use more advanced facilities. The decoders that are replaced in this way can often be used as function only decoders or sold to help finance the upgrade. Alternatively you may wish to start with high specification decoders. Either way the installation process is the same.

Many guides to decoder installation suggest that you should remove the suppression devices, such as chokes and capacitors, from locomotives as part of the process. These components are there to stop the models generating electromagnetic radiation that can interfere with electrical and electronic items ranging from televisions and computers through to police radios and pacemakers. These components have been installed in order that the locomotive will comply with current EU legislation.

Chokes should always be left in place as they do not affect the operation of the decoder. With some installations the capacitors can cause poor or erratic running. Some modern decoders contain RF suppression components in the decoder and so the locomotive's capacitors can be removed. Others do not and in such cases the locomotive's capacitors should be retained. You should refer to the decoder manufacturer's instructions to find out the specific recommendation for each decoder. The best approach appears to be to leave the capacitors in place and remove them only if the locomotive's performance under DCC is poor or erratic when compared to its performance prior to conversion.

Before you begin any installation work you should ensure that the locomotive that you are converting to DCC operates well under conventional DC. Putting a decoder in will not cure a bad motor, binding gears or bent valve gear. Old locomotives should be cleaned and serviced before conversion. Ideally new locomotives should be run in – remember in many cases installing a DCC decoder will involve you in work that will invalidate the manufacturer's warranty, so make sure that the locomotive is not faulty in any way before you start.

It is a good idea to keep a record of what type of decoder you have fitted in each locomotive and what your CV settings are. This will enable you to reset the CV settings if they get changed by accident. A sample DCC locomotive record sheet is provided at the back of this book.

Whilst some locomotives can be converted to DCC easily, others can be challenging. An increasing number of model shops and individuals are offering DCC conversion services and if you are nervous about converting a particular model then you may wish to use such a service. Whilst this does push the cost of the conversion up, it does guarantee that you will get a working DCC locomotive.

Whilst it is imperative that decoders are insulated from the chassis, pick-ups and motor, it is not advisable to cover them with heat shrink tubing or insulating tape. Many decoders generate heat and if it cannot escape into the air they may overheat and cease to work. Some manufacturers supply decoders wrapped in a plastic coating; these are

A decoder supplied wrapped in plastic, in this case a ZTC item.

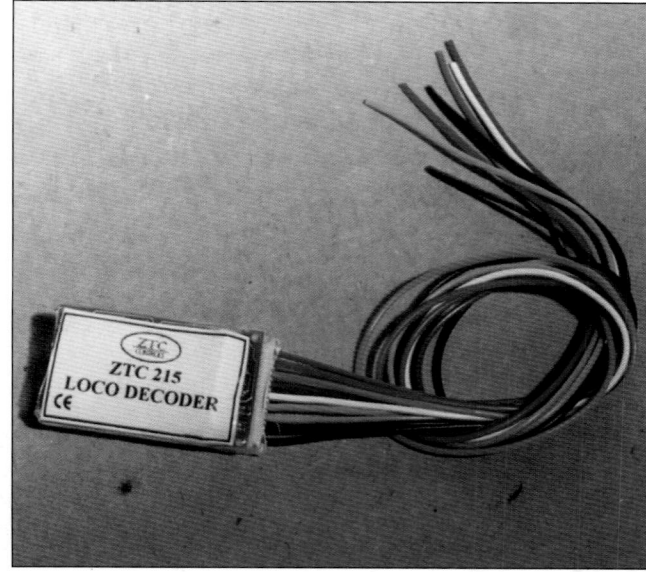

fine and have been designed that way but if your chosen decoder is not wrapped, leave it like that.

Tools of the Trade

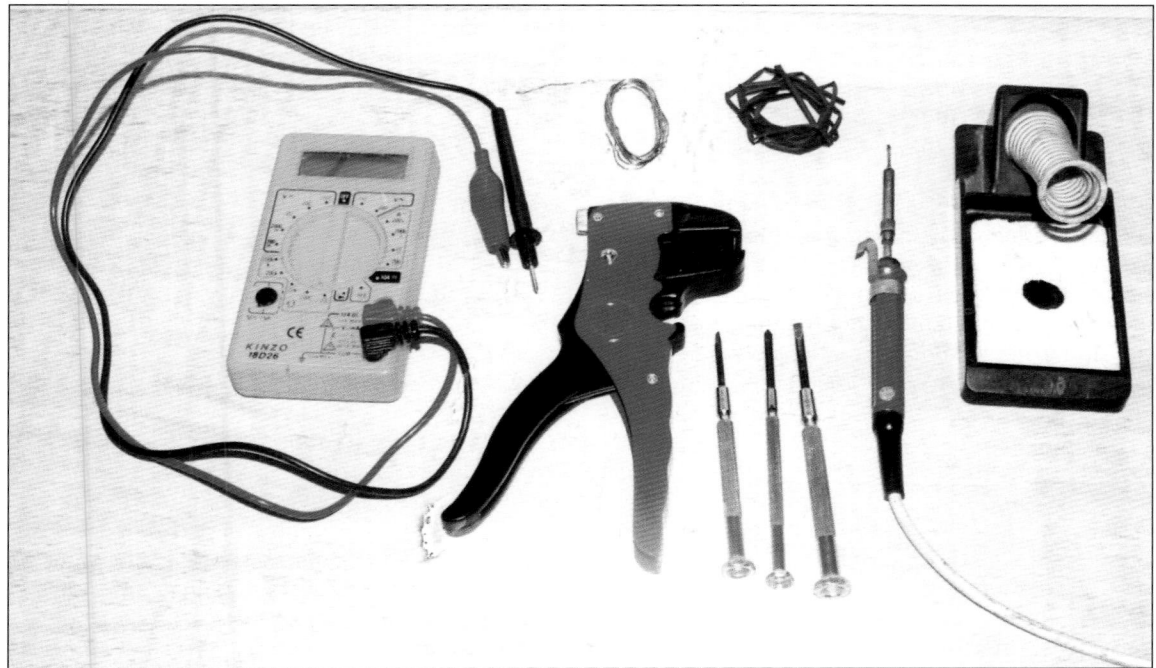

The tools needed to install DCC decoders in your locomotives. Clockwise from the left: electrical meter, solder, heat shrink tubing, soldering iron stand, soldering iron, small screwdrivers and wire strippers.

You will need a small selection of tools and materials to install decoders in your locomotives.

- Electrical meter which can give a resistance (ohm) reading. These will normally also offer other measurements, typically AC and DC voltage (volts) and current (amps). A simple one priced at around £10 or less is perfectly adequate for the job and is invaluable for solving electrical problems on any model railway.
- Wire strippers. Using proper wire strippers is far superior to attempting to strip the insulation with a knife. The strippers ensure that the insulation is removed cleanly and leave all the wire strands intact. There is also no danger of the knife slipping and cutting your finger.
- Small screwdrivers. For removing locomotive bodies and other assorted parts.
- Soldering iron. An electrical soldering iron with a small bit is needed for making electrical connections. If you also need to solder whitemetal kits you should use a different bit (or even a different iron) as electrical and whitemetal solders do not mix well.
- Soldering iron stand. You should have somewhere safe to put your soldering iron when you are not actually using it to make a connection. A purpose designed stand means that there is less chance of a hot soldering iron escaping. As an aside, never try to catch a falling soldering iron. The power cable will tend to make it fall with the hot bit uppermost which is where you will be most likely to grab it, leading to badly burnt fingers. The alternative tactic of trying to catch the lead will cause the iron to swing in an arc and burn you somewhere else. Let it drop and then retrieve it quickly.
- Solder. Electrical solder has the flux incorporated in it.
- Heat shrink tubing. Used to cover bare wires and stop accidental short circuits. Can be obtained from electronics suppliers such as Maplin Electronics and Rapid Electronics.

Joining two wires

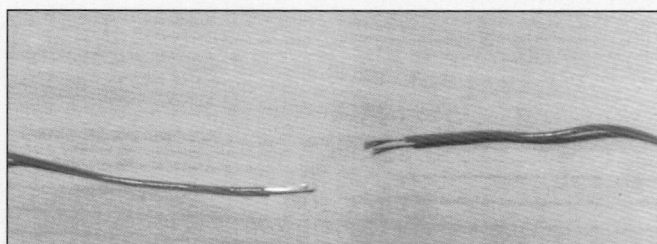

To make a good electrical and mechanical connection between two wires is a simple process. First you strip about a centimetre of insulation from each of the wires to be joined.

Cut a length of heat shrink tubing a little longer than the longest of the bare sections of wire and thread it on to one of the lengths of wire. Now twist the two bare wires together.

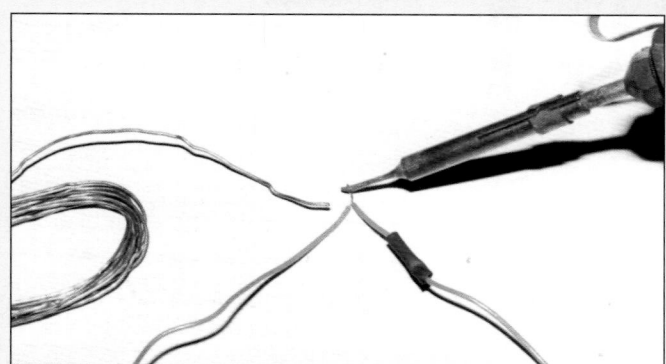

Put the hot soldering iron on the twisted wires and let them heat up. With the soldering iron still in place touch the end of the solder to the twisted wires (not the soldering iron). The solder will melt and flow around the wires. Remove the solder and the iron and allow the joint to cool.

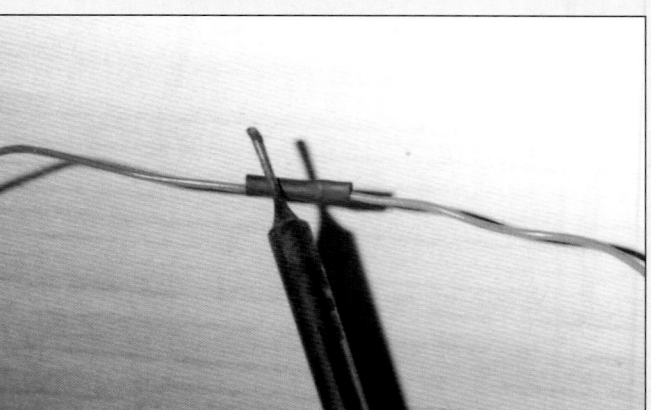

Bend the soldered joint so that it runs parallel to one of the wires. Slide the heat shrink tubing along until it completely covers the soldered joint. Now hold your soldering iron alongside the tubing which will shrink and encase the soldered joint.

You now have a connection that will conduct electricity, resist being pulled apart and not be susceptible to short circuits if it comes into contact with other connections.

Bachmann Class 24 Diesel

DCC-ready diesel locomotives, like the Bachmann Class 24, are the easiest models to convert to DCC operation. Like many modern 4mm scale diesel models this one comes with a DCC socket so that upgrading to DCC is a simple process. I chose to use the Lenz LE1000E decoder which is a basic model that is available quite cheaply. The decoder has a 1A rating, 2 or 4 digit addressing, a full choice of speed steps, analogue (DC) operation, two function outputs and the all-important plug. The only tool that you will need is a small crosshead screwdriver.

If your locomotive is new then make sure that you run it in before starting the conversion. If it is older then consider cleaning and lubricating the mechanism whilst you have the body off. After all, the better it runs on analogue DC the better it will run with DCC.

The body of the Class 24 is held on by four screws that are located underneath the chassis either side of the central belly tanks. You will need to move the bogies to get easy access to them. Once they have all been removed you can turn the locomotive back up the right way and gently ease the body up and off. Don't forget to make a note of which way around the body goes – the number one end (with the roof fan) should go forwards when forward is selected and is the end that goes by the decoder socket.

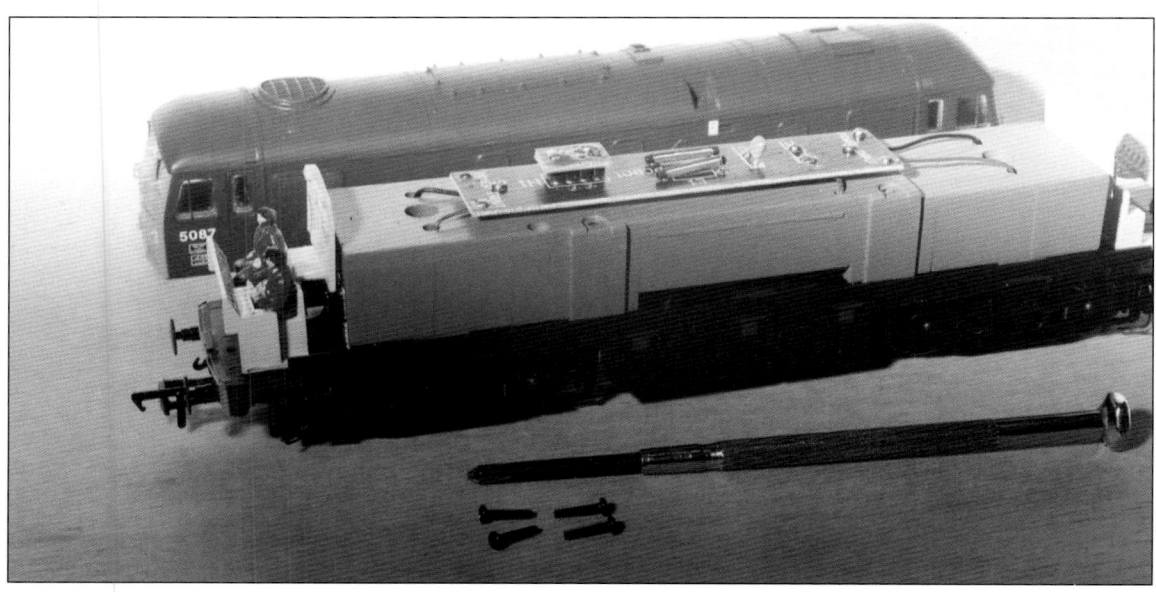

Once the body of the Bachmann Class 24 has been removed, the circuit board where a DCC decoder can be plugged in is easily visible. Remember to check which way the body fits so that the number one end (with the roof fan) ends up at the front when going forwards.

Once the body is off you will see the circuit board with a blanking plug in the DCC socket. Gently remove the plug and put it somewhere safe, just in case you ever want to convert the loco back to analogue operation. Now you can plug the decoder in. Pin 1 is at the front end of the locomotive, so the orange wire needs to be at that end. If you plug the decoder in the wrong way round it will not damage anything – the locomotive will just go backwards instead of forwards.

The next step is to test the decoder installation on the programming track. Temporarily fix it in place with Blu-Tack or something similar, making sure that the circuit board does not touch any metal on the chassis or track. Inadvertent short circuits where the decoder touches a metal part can destroy decoders.

There is plenty of space for the decoder which is secured in place with a double-sided self-adhesive pad.

Once you have tested the decoder on the programming track you can stick it in place using the double-sided adhesive pad that came with it and replace the body. Make sure that you don't catch the wires in the side of the body and that everything slips back together easily. Don't force anything – if it won't fit, take the chassis out and check what the problem is. Fix the body back in place with the four screws and the conversion is complete.

Bachmann Ivatt 4MT

The Bachmann 4MT is described as DCC-ready but is a little harder to convert than their Class 24. Once again the only tool that you need is a small screwdriver.

An increasing number of steam locomotives are now coming fitted with a DCC socket so that upgrading to DCC is a simple process. Once again I chose to use the Lenz LE1000E decoder. The only tool that you will need is a small screwdriver.

You need to work around the brake rigging underneath the loco to remove the front and rear securing screws and then gently remove the body, taking care with the plastic pipework under the cab sides.

The body is secured by two screws. Once these have been removed you can gently ease the body off to reveal the DCC plug on a circuit board under the chimney. This is actually harder than it sounds as the two screws that secure the chassis are underneath some of the plastic brake gear which must be gently eased to one side. The body is a stiff fit and some of the pipework below the cab on the right-hand side of the engine is attached to the body, the rest to the chassis.

The decoder socket is on a small circuit board situated over the front cylinders. Test the installation before putting the model back together.

You can now remove the dummy plug, and put it somewhere safe, then plug in the decoder. Put the chassis on the programming track and check that the decoder responds correctly. Make sure that the decoder doesn't touch any metal parts of the chassis, motor or track whilst you do this.

To make room for the decoder you need to remove the weight from the boiler. This is secured by a small screw. Again, put them somewhere safe in case you ever want to convert the model back to analogue operation. Tuck the decoder into the smokebox and you are ready to put the body back on. Once again this needs care as the pipework at the side of the cab is difficult to get back into position.

Bachmann B1

Bachmann steam locomotives which have a split frame chassis are amongst the harder types to convert for DCC operation. Each side of the chassis is electrically live and separated by insulated spacers. This type of conversion is not recommended for your first attempt.

The first step is to remove the body so that you can check where you are going to put the decoder. In this case I decided to put the decoder in the tender, where there is plenty of room. Other options would be in the cab or to cut away part of the weight in the boiler.

The wheels, valve gear and cylinders can be removed as a complete assembly.

Unscrewing the chassis retaining plate will enable you to lift out the wheels, valve gear and cylinders as a complete unit.

The two sides of the chassis are held together by three screws.

The chassis block is held together by three screws. Once these have been removed the two halves can be separated. Be aware that the insulating spacers that keep the two halves of the chassis electrically isolated may well fall out while you do this, so work over a surface where you can see them drop rather than the carpet!

Once you have separated the two halves of the chassis, and put the various spacers, screws and other parts away safely, you can turn your attention to the motor. Instead of being fed through the chassis it needs to be fed by wires which will be connected to the decoder. The motor's terminals and the wires need to be electrically isolated from the chassis.

As we are putting the decoder in the tender we need separate wires to carry the motor and track voltages from the locomotive to the tender. You can buy fine, flexible wire suitable for decoder connections from model railway shops or electronics suppliers. I salvaged some wires from a discarded computer mouse. If you strip the outer casing away you will find four thin, flexible cables that can be used for projects like this one. One drawback is that the colours from the mouse cable do not match the colours on the decoder wires, so you must make a note of which colour wire does what for future reference.

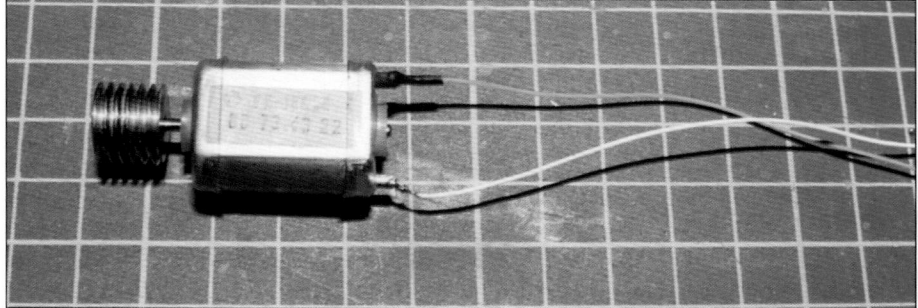

Solder one wire to each of the motor terminals and then cover the terminal and end of the wire with heat shrink tubing. Make sure that the terminal is completely covered.

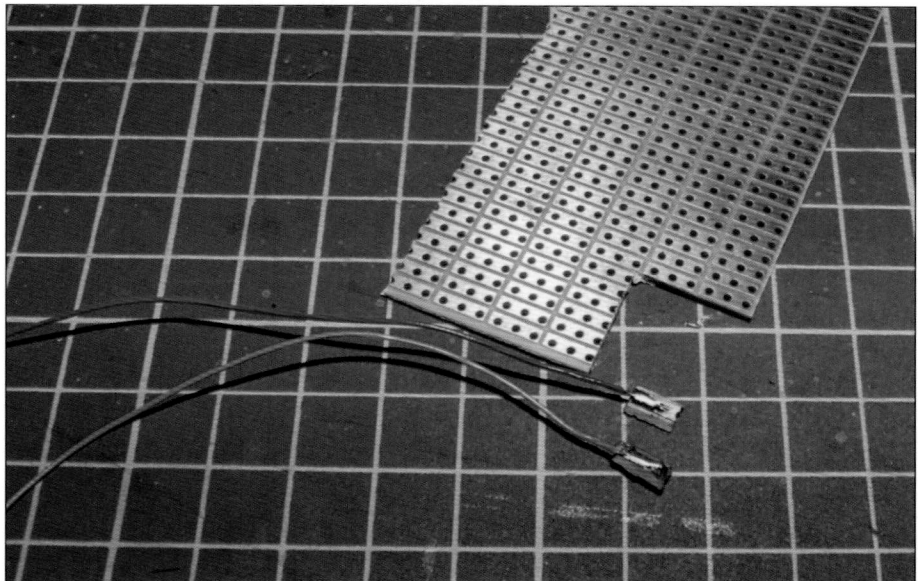

To make the pick-ups you need to use some copper-clad paxolin. This is used as sleepers for soldered track or for making electronic circuits. If you purchase a small piece of stripboard or copper-clad board you can cut pieces off it as required with a razor saw. Cut two small pieces and solder a wire to each.

Scrape off some of the black coating from the inside of the chassis blocks where you will be taking the electrical pick-up. Reassemble the chassis, but do not tighten it up yet. You may find it useful to hold some of the parts in place with Blu-Tack or a similar product to cut down on the number of hands you need to do this. Slip the two pieces of copperclad board in place where the chassis block coating has been scraped away. The two pieces should have the copper side facing outwards, one to each side.

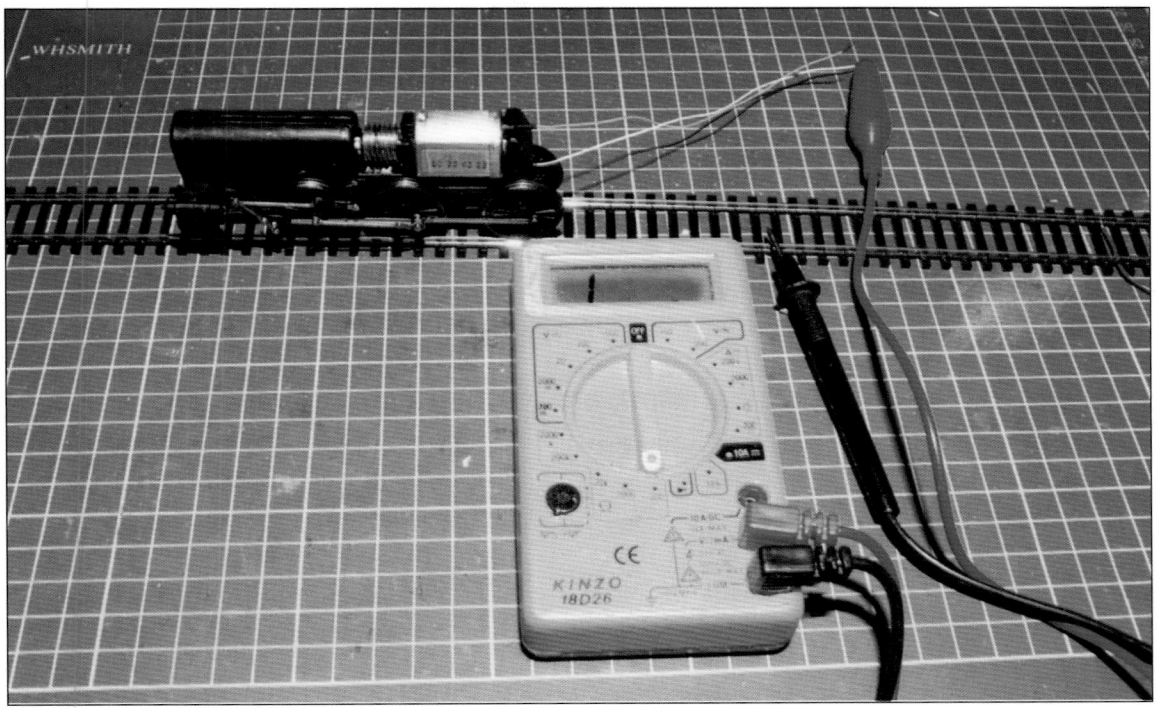

Now check that all four wires are electrically isolated from each other using the multimeter. If you find a problem, correct it. You should also check that the two wires from the copperclad board are electrically connected to the track and that the motor wires are not.

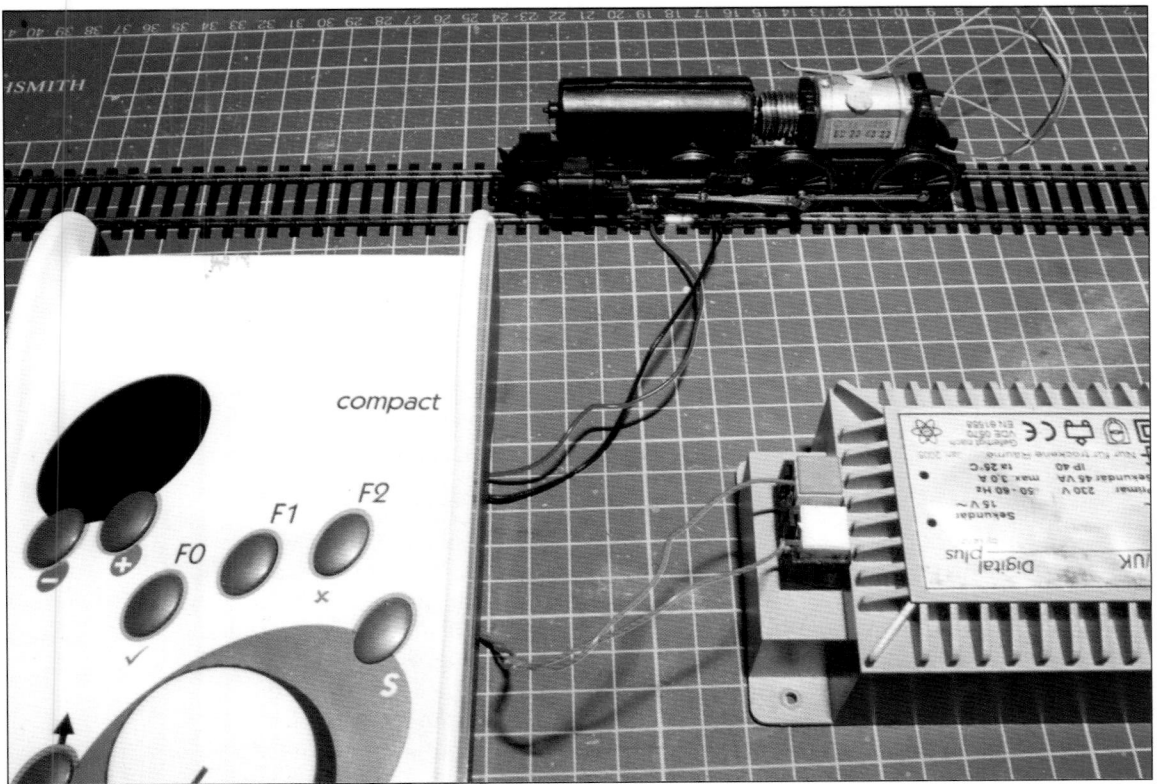

A final check under analogue control before fitting the DCC decoder will make sure that your electrical connections are working properly.

Once you are happy with the wires you can temporarily join the track wires to the motor wires and check that you have assembled the chassis correctly by test running it on analogue DC. You can either use a DC controller or a DCC controller in analogue mode. Remember that you need to get the chassis running smoothly before you fit the decoder.

Attention now turns to the tender. The weights were moved back slightly to clear space for a hole in the chassis so that the wires could get inside. A screw terminal block, intended for mounting on an electronic circuit board, was fixed to the rear end of the tender. This will enable the wires from the locomotive and the decoder to be disconnected for maintenance and changing the decoder if necessary.

The wires from the locomotive were cut to length. A small fold of insulating tape around the wires inside the tender will stop them being pulled out through the hole when the locomotive is handled. The decoder wires were coiled. Not cutting the decoder wires keeps all your options open if you ever swap the decoder into another locomotive.

The DCC decoder is connected to a terminal block in the tender. The wires from the locomotive run through a hole in the tender chassis to the terminal block.

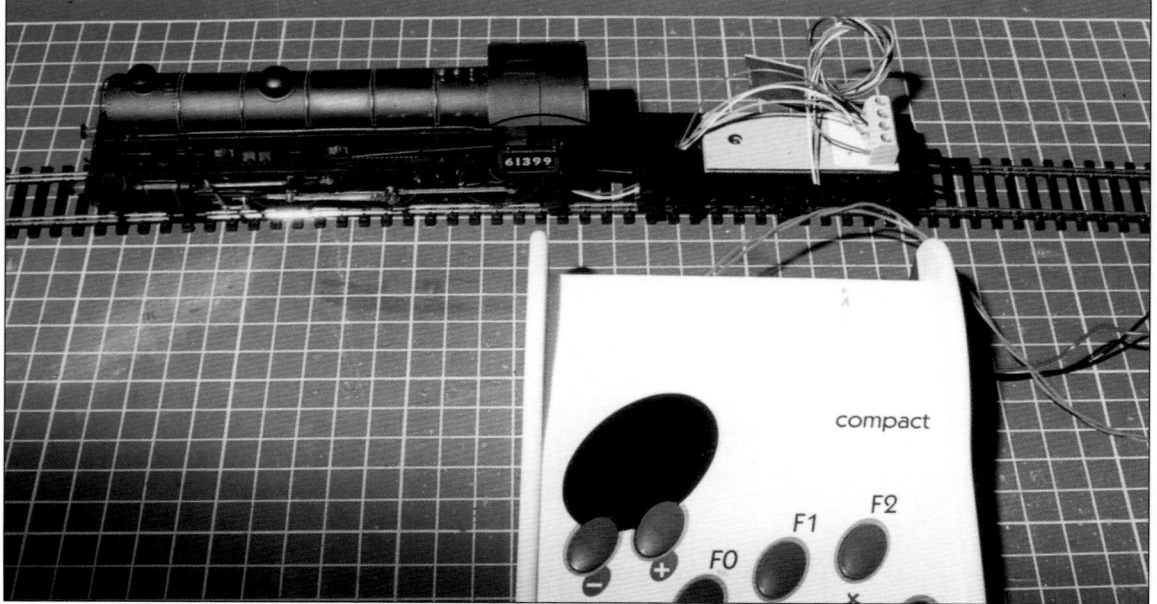

Next comes a test on the programming track, and if all is in working order the decoder can be stuck down on its sticky pad and the tender body reattached. As an extra touch the visible length of the wires between the locomotive and tender could be painted black to make them less obvious.

Graham Farish Class 08 Shunter ('N' gauge)

The Graham Farish Class 08 shunter has been around for many years and makes an ideal example of how a decoder can be squeezed into even a small model. Given that there is not a great deal of space with which to work, a small decoder is a must. I opted for the TCS M1 but the ZTC-213 would also be eminently suitable. The photo on page 38 shows the difference in size between the TCS M1 (left) and a Lenz LE100 decoder. Trying to fit a normal sized decoder into a locomotive this size would be just about impossible.

Whilst it is normal to have four or more function outputs on decoders intended for 4mm scale models, some decoders designed for N scale models have only two. This is not such a hardship as it may at first seem as there is far less scope for fitting complex lighting and other accessories to locomotives in this scale. By the time that you have got a suitable weight, motor and decoder in the body there is unlikely to be very much room left. The TCS M1 has two functions, whilst the ZTC-213 has four. As there is no lighting installed in the Graham Farish 08 we do not need any functions at all.

The TCS M1 is 0.35" wide, 0.565" long and 0.125" thick and so is small enough to fit in the model's cab. Whilst it is small in size, the decoder has a number of advanced features including automatically converting to DC operation, 'dither' capability for excellent slow speed running, 2 and 4 digit addressing, 'on the main' programming and, as a bonus, a 'no questions asked' replacement warranty.

Even with a small decoder such as this, it is still difficult to find space inside the body. The M1 is a snug fit inside the cab. Always check that your chosen decoder fits in its intended location before you start work; it is better to have to revise your plans at this stage rather than after you have unsoldered wires or modified the chassis.

On many Graham Farish locomotives the lower of the engine brushes is directly connected to the chassis block which is electrically live. Attempting to separate the chassis and brush electrically is a difficult process. The top brush is mounted in a plastic housing and is easily dealt with, whereas the lower brush is seated in the chassis. Fortunately the problem can be solved using a couple of specially produced parts from Gerry Spencer.

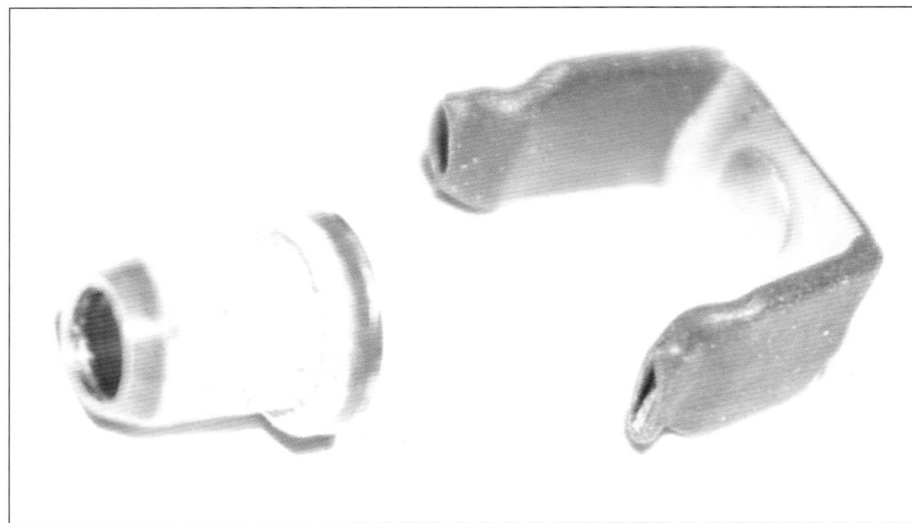

The conversion kit costs around £10 and includes a modified brush guide, modified retaining clip and a specially sized drill. The new brush guide is insulated and fits in the existing hole in the chassis once it has been opened out with the specially sized drill. The new retaining clip needs to be soldered to one of the DCC decoder motor leads. The other motor lead is soldered to the other brass clip. One of the track leads is soldered to the long bolt carrying power from one side of the chassis, and the other to the chassis itself. Check the installation on your programming track and then refit the body.

Hornby Pannier Tank

This is an example of one of the many old locomotives that are still giving service on layouts up and down the country. Whilst it might seem strange to fit a decoder that may cost more than the locomotive is worth, this must be judged against the cost of a modern replacement loco and, quite possibly, the retirement of a favourite model. I should point out that the current Hornby tank locomotive chassis is to a different design. The motor is fed from wires so DCC conversion is simply a matter of connecting the pick-up wires to the decoder and the decoder to the motor. Older versions of this chassis, however, can present difficulties.

Sometimes the chassis securing screws can be ingeniously hidden. To get at the screw in this Hornby pannier tank you have to remove the tank top which clips in place.

On this model you need to remove the top of the pannier tank in order to access the screw to remove the chassis.

The tank provides an ideal place to hide a decoder, making sure that it does not obstruct the chassis retaining screw.

Having got the chassis out you can then examine the electrical connections. On one side there are electrical pick-ups that wipe against the back of the wheels. Current is taken through a wire to the RF suppression components and the motor. On the other side current flows through the wheels and axles to the chassis and thence to the motor. I must admit that I spent a long time trying to work out how to isolate the motor from the chassis before I realised how to fit the decoder.

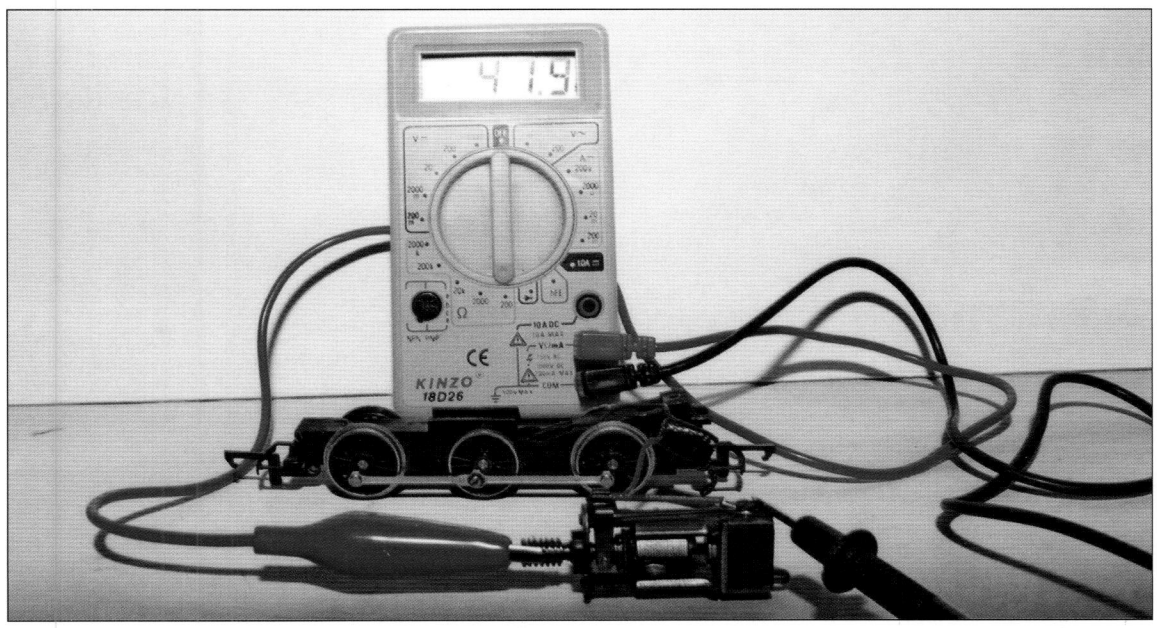

Sometimes you can spend a lot of time and effort working out how to fit a decoder. Here a meter is being used to establish which parts of the motor are electrically live.

The secret is to insulate the wire spring that holds the brushes in place. One arm is already insulated and by insulating the other arm the motor brushes can be quickly and easily isolated from the chassis. There are a number of ways to do this. You can cut the sleeving from the right-hand arm in half, use insulated sleeving stripped from a wire or heat shrink tubing.

Once both motor brushes have been isolated it is simple to fit the decoder. The grey and orange leads go to the brushes whilst the red and black ones go to the pick-up.

Unsolder the red pick-up wire from the right-hand brush and connect it to the decoder's red wire. Solder the decoder's orange wire to the right-hand brush. The decoder's grey wire needs to be soldered to the left-hand brush. Finally the decoder's black wire should be soldered to the tag on the motor retaining screw. The capacitor attached to the tag can be removed and the installation tested with a meter before you place the loco on the programming track.

Hornby Class 52 'Western' Diesel

Like many Hornby models the 'Western' is powered by a 'Ringfield' motor. These can be found in diesel motor bogies, tank engines and steam engine tenders. They are all to a similar pattern and have been part of the hobby for more years than most people care to remember. For this installation I have used a ZTC 215 Budget Decoder.

The Western comes with at least two versions of the 'Ringfield' motor, which require slightly different treatment. The first step (after you have made sure that the model is working on standard DC) is to dismantle it and see what you are dealing with.

First you need to remove one of the bogies by levering the rear retaining lug forwards with a small screwdriver. The bogie can then be lifted out. The body is held in place by a series of lugs. You can now push from inside to release one end of the body and then run a fingernail along the gap releasing the rest of the lugs as you go. Once the body is off you can detach the second bogie in exactly the same way as the first one.

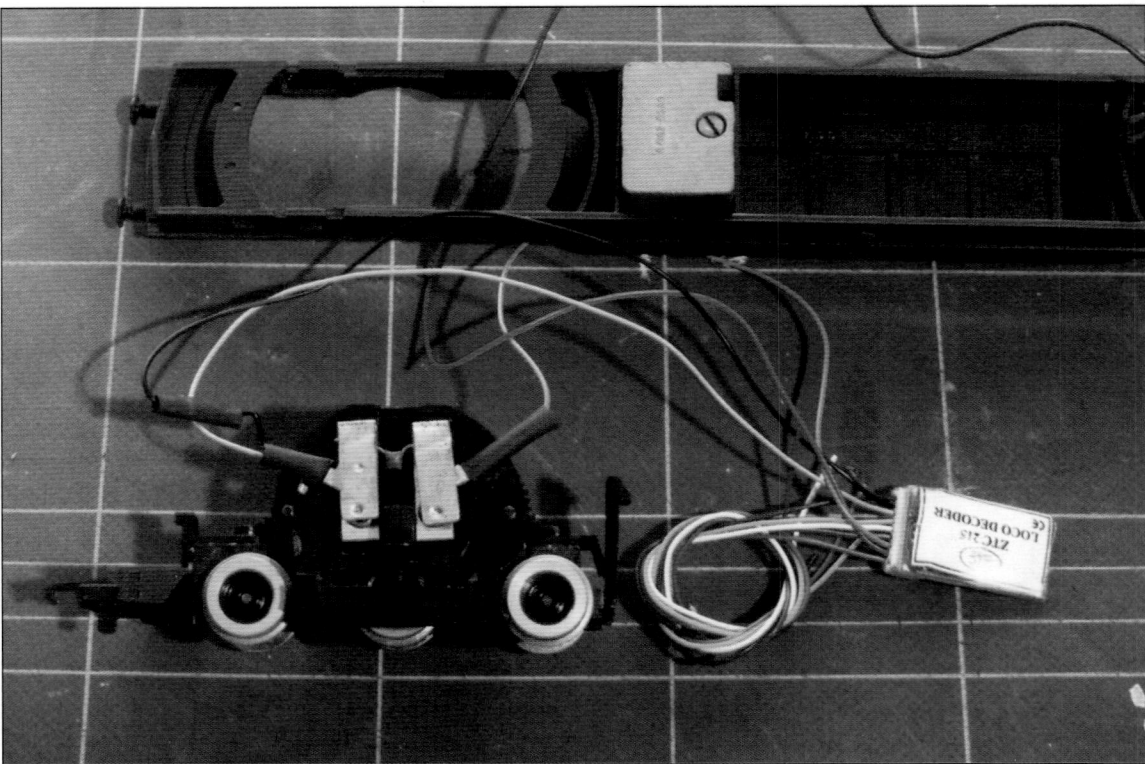

If your motor bogie does not have screws at the top of the brush holders, like the one above, then fitting the decoder is a simple matter.

Disconnect the two wires from the motor, attach them to the red and black decoder wires and then solder the orange and grey wires to the tags on the motor.

You can then test the installation, stick the decoder down in the well of the chassis and reassemble the model.

Motor bogies that have two screws at the top of the brush holders need more extensive work. Some motors have two connections to pick-ups, others only have one. In both cases there is a hidden connection that enables the motor to collect power from one side of the motor bogie. If you fail to disconnect this then your decoder will be destroyed the first time that you try to use it.

Looking at the motor bogie on page 45 there are two screws which keep the brush holders in place. The one on the right is perfectly normal, but the one on the left is longer and connects the brush holder to the chassis and thence to the track.

First you must remove the left-hand screw. You need a solder tag and insulating washer to fit. Connect the solder tag to the decoder's black wire (track pick-up). If the left-hand brush retainer is also connected to a wire then that wire needs to be unsoldered and connected to the decoder's black wire. Now unsolder the other pick-up from the right-hand brush holder and connect to the decoder's red wire.

The grey wire can now be soldered to the left-hand brush holder and the orange wire to the right-hand one. Place the solder tag on the screw, followed by the insulating washer and then replace the screw. Make sure that the solder tag does not make contact with the brush holder or the chassis.

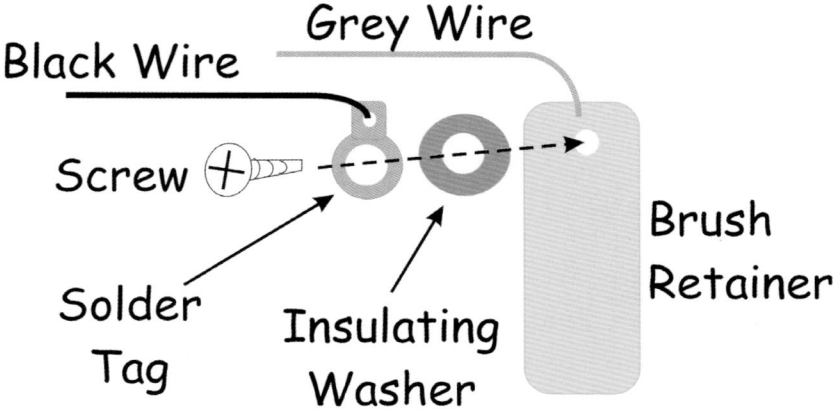

You can either make your own solder tags from brass strip or purchase them from Maplin Electronics, Rapid Electronics or Squires Model & Craft Tools. Similarly plastic sheet can be used to make suitable insulating washers, and can be shaped to ensure there is no possibility of the solder tag touching the motor, or you can purchase them from Rapid Electronics or Squires Model & Craft Tools.

Lima Class 117 DMU

Whilst Lima are no longer in business, there are many thousands of locomotives that were produced by them around. Most UK outline models produced by Lima used the same design of motor bogie, so these instructions apply equally well to virtually all Lima models. The only difference will be in locating a suitable place to install the decoder.

Incidentally, the Lima motor is not highly regarded due to its lack of controllability and reliability. You may wish to replace the motor with a different unit, such as the Black Beetle powered bogie available from Branchlines. There is also a kit available from the Australian company ModelTorque that converts the existing Lima motor into a much higher specification item which is ideal for those who do not wish to make any structural changes to the model's chassis. The kit is available direct from the manufacturer or from The Engine Shed and Inter-City Models in the UK.

The body of the Lima Class 117 DMU is clipped rather than screwed in place. To release it you need to use a small screwdriver to release each clip in turn until you can lift the body off the chassis.

With the interior visible through the coach windows there appears to be limited space to conceal a decoder. The bulkhead between the guard's and passenger sections provides a suitable place to secure a Lenz L1000A decoder.

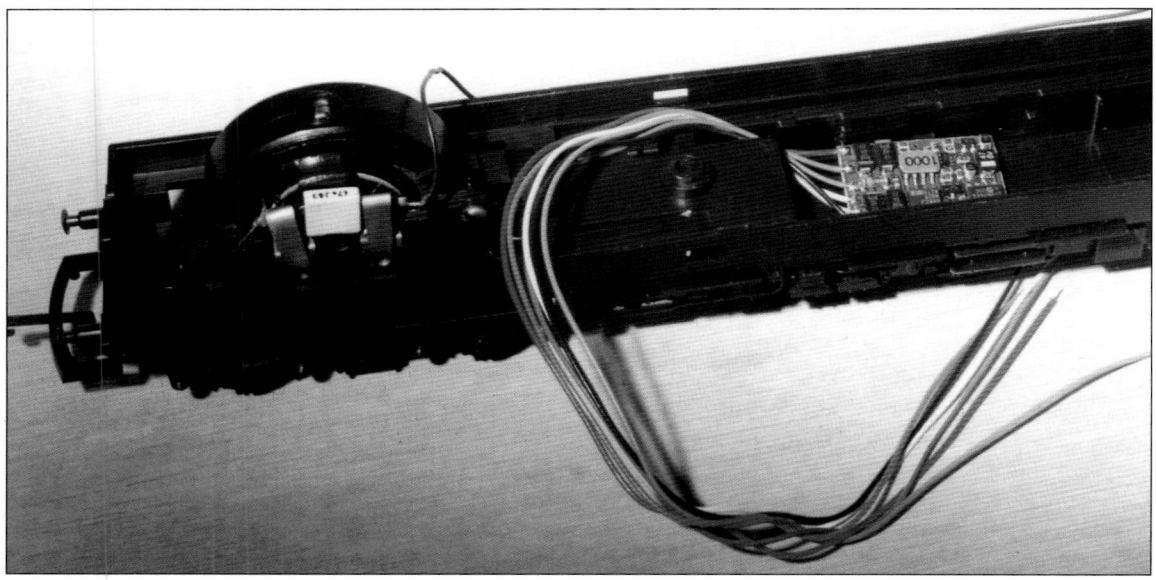

As with many diesel models the belly tanks provide a large space where a decoder can be completely concealed, even a large one with sound and a speaker. Once you have decided where the decoder is going to go you can disconnect the feed from the front bogie (it just pulls off the central pivot) and remove the motor bogie by unscrewing the outer frame.

The short wire connecting the motor bogie pick-up to one motor terminal should be unsoldered and discarded. The black pick-up wire from the other bogie should be unsoldered and retained. You can now solder the DCC decoder's motor wires to the motor terminals and the decoder's track wires to the motor bogie pick-up and the black pick-up wire. Any function wires should be insulated with heat shrink sleeving to stop them causing any problems later.

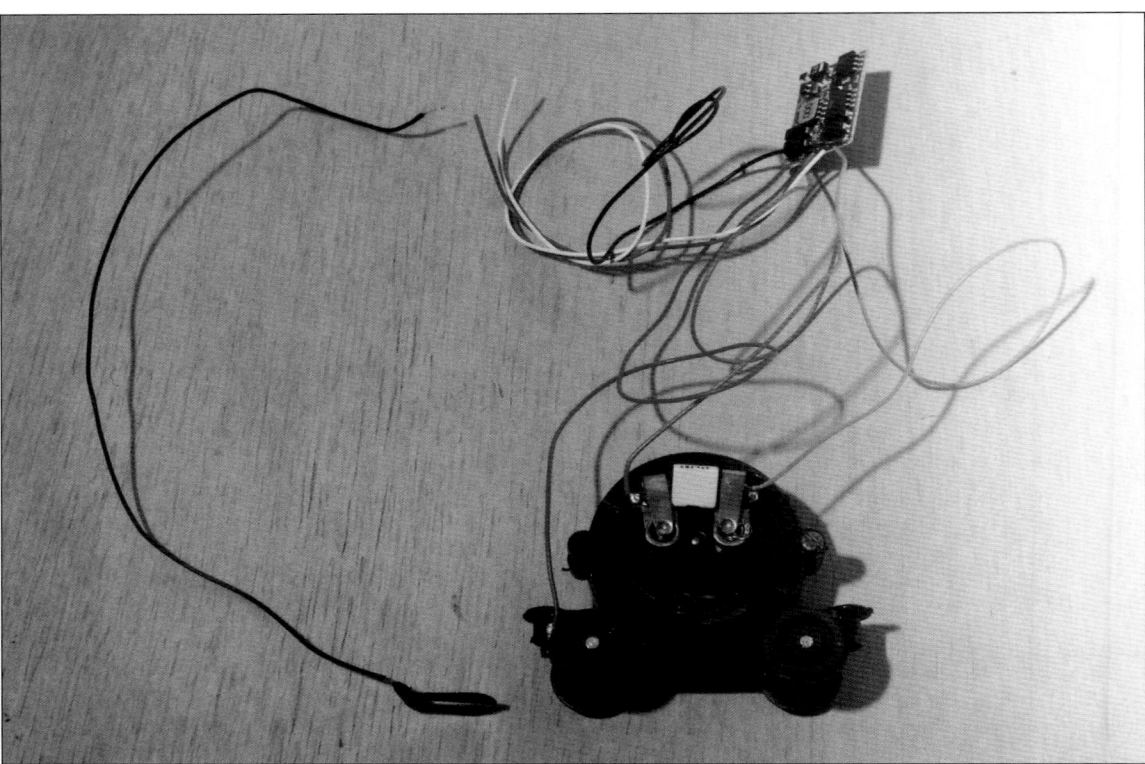

The motor bogie can now be temporarily reconnected to the pick-up bogie and the installation tested on the programming track. If there are no problems the decoder can be fixed in place and the model reassembled.

Accessory Decoders

DCC can not only control your track and locomotives but also points, signals and other accessories. Accessory decoders come in a variety of types for different purposes. As they have to control everything from street lights to solenoid point motors this is hardly surprising. Most accessory decoders can control four different items and many can operate a mix of devices.

Controlling the accessories is normally handled by your command station. Most command stations will allow you to control individual accessories and many allow you to set up 'routes'. A route is a selection of accessories, such as points and signals, that are set at the same time. This allows you to set all the points and signals for a manoeuvre with a single operation. As you can imagine, the saving in time and reduction of errors on even a medium sized layout makes this worth considering.

One common misconception is that you cannot use the same numbers for points or routes as you can for locomotives. This is not true. The two types of decoders each have their own range of addresses so you can have both a locomotive number 1 and a point number 1. The cab should make it clear which one you are trying to operate at any given time.

Running your accessory decoders can cause problems on large layouts. The high current draw needed to operate twin solenoid point motors can lead to a momentary loss of power if a large number of trains or accessories are in operation. Also if a locomotive causes a short circuit by running into a point that is set against it this will shut down the control station and thus you will be unable to change the point to remove the short. It is far better to feed the accessories from a separate bus fed from either its own cut out or a separate booster.

Route Setting

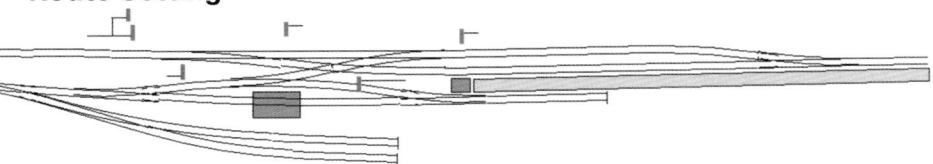

A single line branch terminus would typically have each point and signal individually controlled by separate switches on the layout's control panel.

Route 1

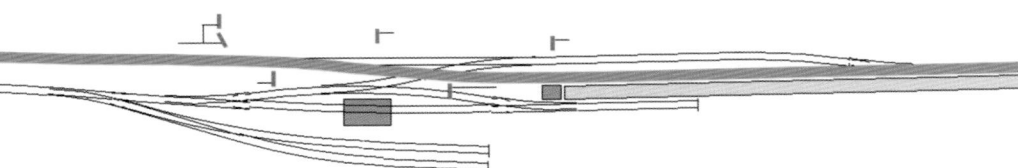

Whilst it is possible to control each point and signal individually under DCC, many command stations have the facilities to set routes. Here the points and signals are set for an arriving passenger train (route 1).

Route 2

A route can still be a single point, as with the route to release an engine from the platform end (route 2).

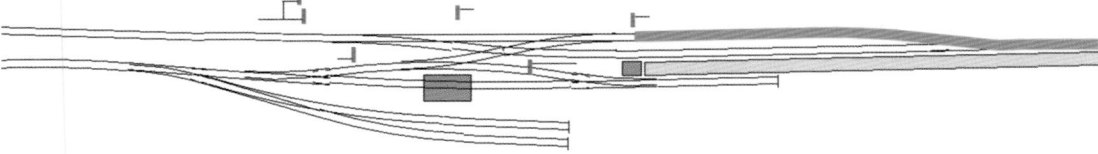

Route 3

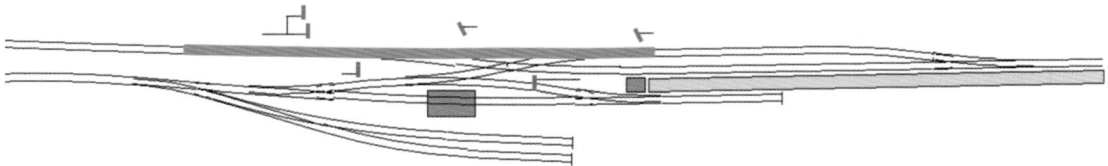

The next route (3) clears the locomotive through the station throat. This would also be the departure route for goods trains which would arrive and depart from the run-round loop. Once the passenger locomotive has cleared the home signal setting route 1 again would allow it to set back onto its train ready for departure.

Route 4

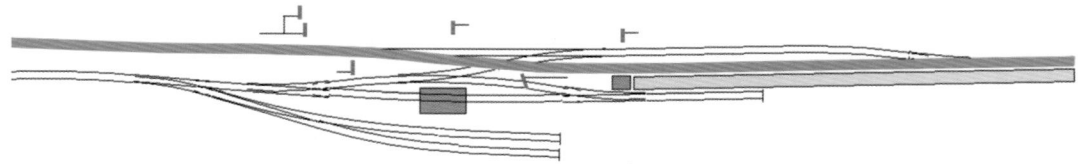

Route 4 is similar to route 1 except that it is signalled for a departing passenger train rather than an arriving one.

Route 5

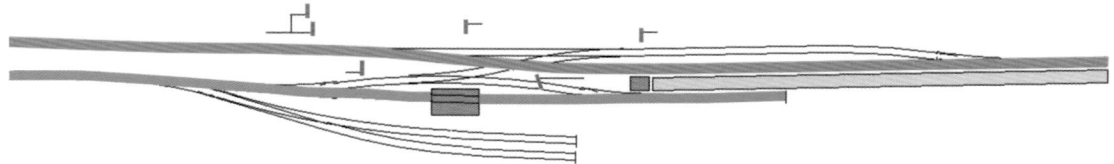

Of course with DCC you can have a locomotive shunting the goods yard at the same time as your passenger train is using the platform line.

Route 6

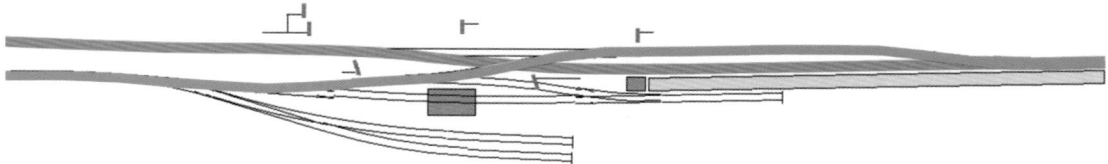

Unfortunately there is nothing in DCC to stop you setting conflicting routes. If you want to have points and signals interlocked you either need to use a specially constructed conventional point and signal control system or operate them via a computer interface and a suitable program.

A Typical Accessory Decoder

Most accessory decoders have four pairs of outputs. These can be used to control point motors, signals, electric uncouplers, lights and many other electrically powered accessories. The four pairs of outputs are numbered in a block so that a decoder may, as an example, use addresses 1 to 4 or 85 to 88.

Each pair of outputs can normally be programmed to give a burst of power or to be continuously on. Both the outputs of a pair have the same setting, but different pairs of outputs can have different settings.

All decoders need to be connected to the track bus in order to pick up the DCC commands; however, some can be connected to a separate power supply.

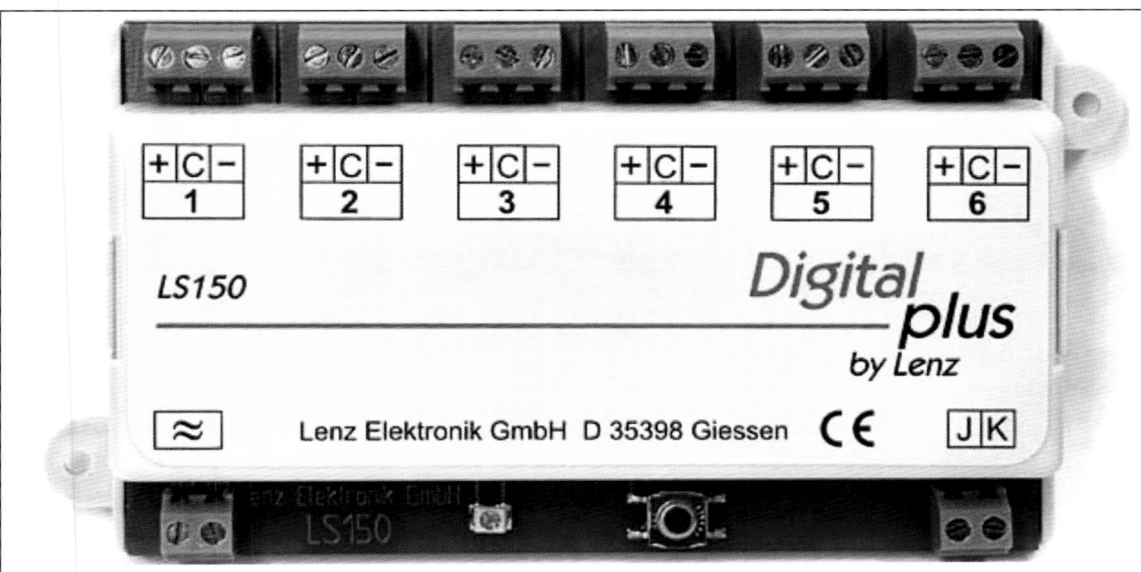

The Lenz LS150 accessory decoder can operate up to six items such as point motors. It provides separate signal and power inputs so that operating heavy current items such as solenoid point motors does not affect the running of trains.

This is very useful if you use solenoid point motors which take a lot of power. Using a separate power supply means that you do not drain the power from the track bus which could cause your locomotives to behave erratically.

The decoder outputs provide either a DC or AC output of around 12-16V. Different devices need to be connected in different ways.

ZTC have introduced a single accessory decoder. The ZTC 303 will operate just about any type of accessory and connects direct to the track or power bus. This is a great benefit where you do not have sufficient items in an area to justify a four or six output decoder.

Twin Coil Solenoid Point Motors

The typical model railway point motor consists of a pair of solenoid coils which need a pulse of electricity to operate them. If they are subjected to a continuous voltage they very quickly burn out.

Most accessory decoders are set to operate this type of point motor as a default.

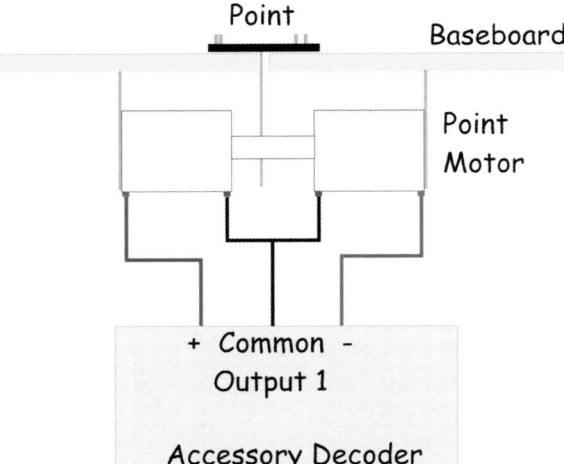

One output is connected to each coil and the common wire is connected to both coils. This is exactly the same method as would be used for conventional operation with push buttons or similar switches. If your point motor has an auxiliary switch and your decoder has a feedback facility the switch can be connected to the decoder so that the point's setting can be read by the command station.

Where two point motors need to be operated at the same time, for example on a crossover, you should not connect both point motors to the same decoder output. Instead you should connect each point motor to its own individual output and set them both to the same address.

A development from the British company ZTC is the ZTC 302 point motor. It can be mounted in place of standard Peco or Hornby point motors and includes its own built-in decoder. This simplifies point motor wiring as only two wires are needed to connect the point motor to the track or power bus rather than the normal three from point motor to decoder and two from the decoder to the track or power bus.

Slow Motion Motors

Slow motion point motors such as the Tortoise or those produced by Fulgurex need to be connected differently to the twin solenoid types. They require a constant DC voltage in one direction or the other to operate and hold the point blades in position.

An increasing number of modellers are now using slow motion point motors, such as this Fulgurex product, to operate points and semaphore signals. Rather than the 'snap' action of conventional twin solenoid motors these motors move the point blades slowly, resulting in a more realistic appearance and less wear on the point.

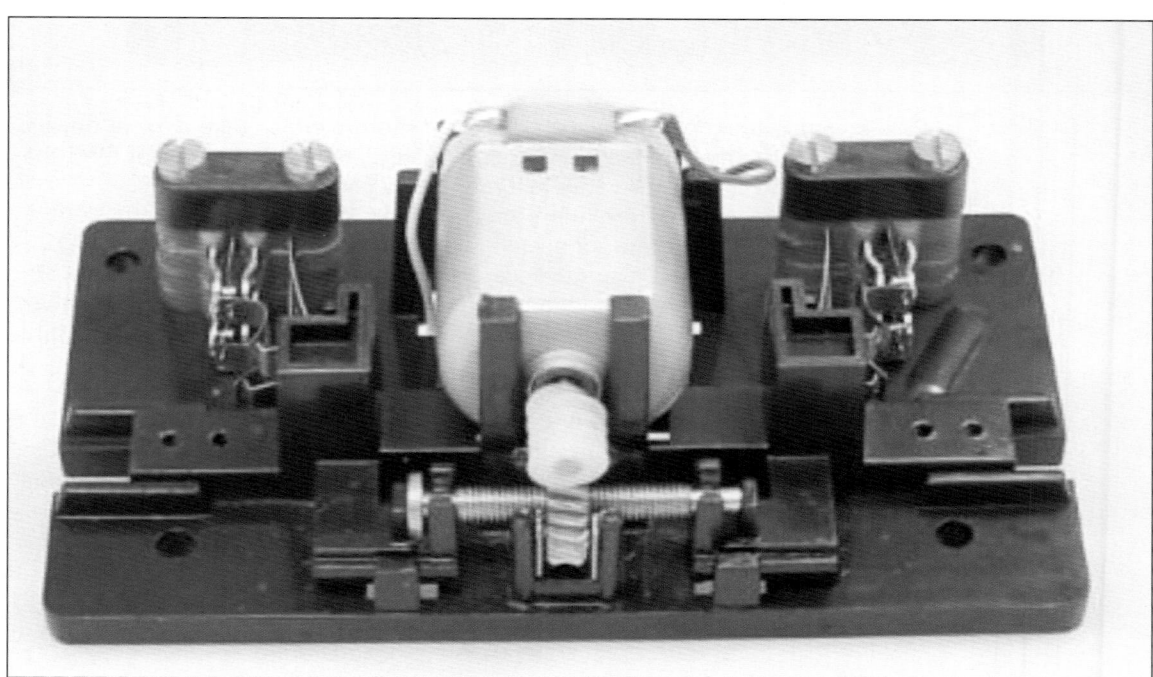

For DC output decoders you need to purchase an extra interface unit that converts the three wire output to a two wire one suitable for driving the motors.

For AC output decoders, such as the Lenz LS150 the interface consists of two standard diodes connected to route opposing polarities to one terminal of the point motor. The other terminal is connected to the common output of the decoder.

Colour Light Signals

Two aspect colour light signals with 12V bulbs can be connected directly to the outputs of the accessory decoder.

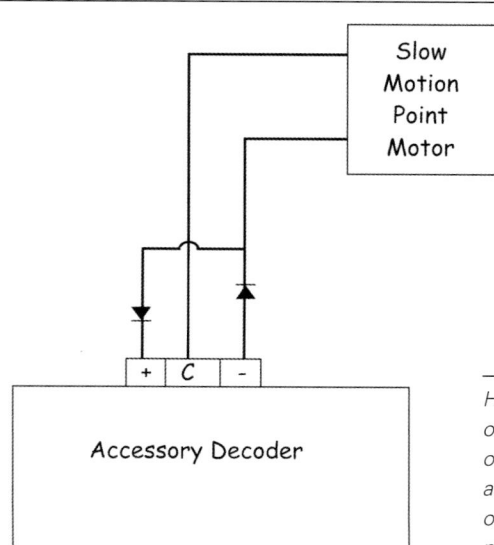

How to convert the output of an AC output decoder such as the Lenz LS150 to operate slow motion point motors.

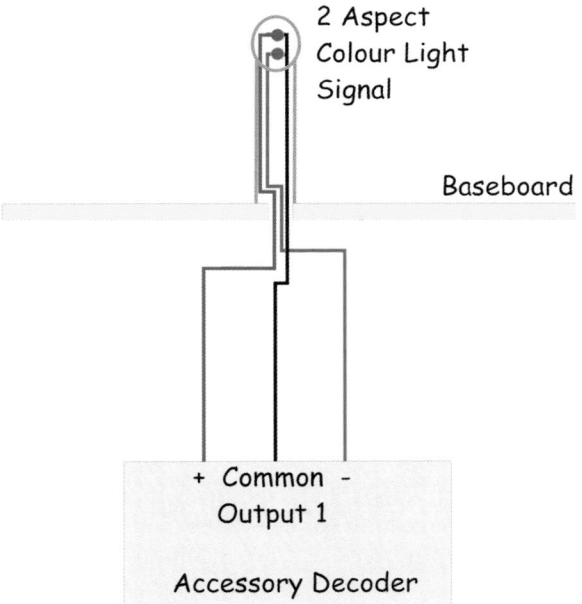

Signals that use LEDs need a current limiting resistor in order to work properly. Note also that the LEDs need to have the anodes connected together and to the common terminal on the decoder. Current flows from the common terminal through the LED to the + or – terminal. If you use LEDs on an AC output decoder (such as the Lenz LS150) you will also need to add a normal diode between the signal and the resistor (with the anode at the resistor end and the cathode at the signal end) to protect the LEDs from the AC voltage.

For a supply voltage of 16V AC the resistor should typically be 1K5Ω rated at 0.25W or greater. If your supply voltage is lower, the LEDs may appear dim and in that case the resistor can be reduced to 1KΩ. If the LEDs are too bright for your needs then they can be dimmed by using a higher value resistor, normally 1K8Ω or 2K2Ω.

Multiple aspect colour light signals cannot be directly operated using an accessory decoder but this accords with prototype practice as on real railways the signals cycle through the different aspects automatically. The signalman can set a signal to red to stop a train and then clear the signal, but the actual aspect that it displays (green, double yellow or yellow) is dependent on the position of other trains on the line.

If you have a multiple aspect colour light system installed then the accessory decoder can act as the signalman's set/clear switch replacing the equivalent control on your signalling panel. To do this it will probably be necessary to connect a relay to the accessory decoder and use the relay contacts to replace the mechanical switch.

Other Accessories

You can, of course, use an accessory decoder to control just about anything that you would normally operate with a switch. Roco produce a DCC operated crane, Heljan make a remarkable container crane and it is easy to connect up lights, level crossings and other animated scenes.

Wiring for DCC

In the introduction I touched on the marketing myth that you need just two wires for DCC. Whilst this does have some truth in it, it is likely that you will need more than that – but a lot less than a conventional analogue DC layout. If you already have your layout wired up then it is possible to reuse that wiring but you may find it beneficial to rewire it. This can, of course, be done in stages over time.

The two most important wires on a DCC layout are usually called the track bus. These are the 'two wires' of mythology. Their job is to distribute the power and DCC signal to the track and anything else that happens to be connected to them.

These should be of thick cable to minimise any loss of power and should, as far as possible, run parallel to each other. Usually they are coloured red and black for easy identification. The track bus is connected to the track by short, thinner wires. Ideally each piece of rail should be connected to one of the bus wires but, as a minimum, the bus wires should be connected to the track at intervals of three to six feet. The table below gives the minimum recommended sizes for bus wires. If you have long wires, in excess of 4m, then you will need to use thicker cable to avoid the track voltage dropping as you get further away from the booster.

Booster Capacity	Bus Cable Size
3A bus	Single core wire – 20AWG
	Stranded wire – 16/0.2mm
	Conductor area (stranded or single core) – 0.5mm²
6A bus	Single core wire – 18AWG
	Stranded wire – 24/0.2mm
	Conductor area (stranded or single core) – 0.75mm²
10A bus	Stranded wire – 32/0.2mm
	Conductor area (stranded or single core) – 1.0mm²

Using overhead catenary can cause short circuits if the locomotive also picks up from both rails. If the locomotive picks up from only one rail (the blue rail in the left-hand illustration) then turning it round will leave it unpowered.

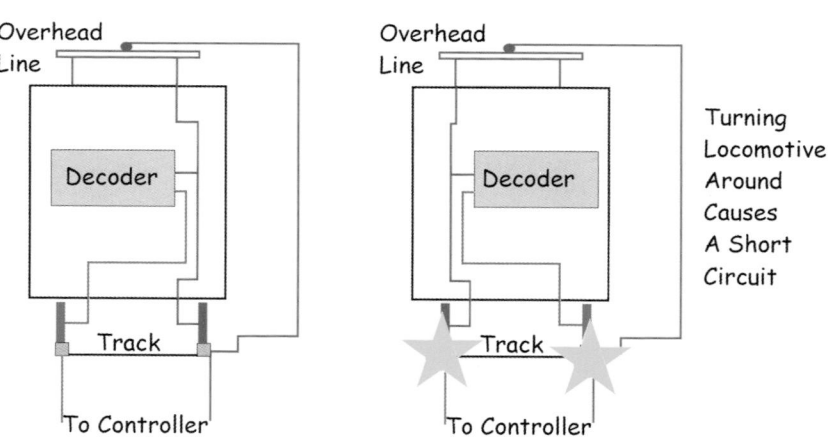

Incidentally it is recommended that DCC is not used for pick-up from overhead wires unless both rails are electrically linked. If the overhead was connected to one of the running rails then turning a locomotive around, either manually or by running around a reverse loop, would cause a short circuit. If you were to use a different booster for the overhead wire to that for the track underneath it then placing a locomotive the 'wrong way round' would lead to double the track voltage being supplied to the decoder which would be destroyed very quickly.

When a short circuit occurs on the layout, for example when a locomotive derails, then the full current from the booster will flow along the bus and through the short. As this will typically be between 2 and 5 amps the booster is fitted with a high speed circuit breaker that detects the sudden current surge and shuts the power off thus preventing any damage to the booster, wiring or locomotives. However, if the bus wires are too thin they can cause the track voltage to drop to such an extent that the booster cannot detect the short circuit and activate the circuit breaker. If that happens and the short is not removed, or the power shut off manually, the short can generate sufficient heat to damage track and rolling stock or even start a fire. You can test if your wiring is good enough to allow the booster to detect a short simply by placing something metal, such as a screwdriver, across the tracks at various places around the layout. The booster should shut down and indicate a short circuit every time. If it doesn't then you will need to increase the size of the bus wires or add extra feeds in the areas where short circuits are not detected.

Inadequate wiring also causes poor performance. Nickel-silver rail has a much higher electrical resistance than copper wire and if there are long runs without feeders from the track bus there will be a significant drop in the voltage at the track. This will cause locomotives to run slowly or even stop as the locomotive's decoder will shut down if there isn't enough power to operate it. This is particularly noticeable if you have locomotives with additional functions such as lights and sound.

Having got your booster to shut down every time that there is a short, you will probably find it very irritating that all trains stop whenever you have a problem. To avoid a derailment in the goods yard stopping the mainline trains you need to have either a number of boosters or electronic cut-outs, each supplying a separate area of the layout. Each booster or cut-out will have its own bus. Do not connect the track buses together as this will defeat the object of having the boosters and could well damage them. There is no need for the track sections attached to a booster to be contiguous. For example, you might have three boosters: one for the up main line, one for the down main line and a third for the locomotive depot on the down side of the station and the goods yard on the up side. A benefit of adding extra boosters is that you have more power available for operating locomotives and accessories such as coaches with interior lighting.

One thing to watch for if you are installing multiple boosters is to ensure that you are consistent with connecting the red and black bus wires in each section. The easiest way to check that you have done this correctly is to use a meter set to its AC volt scale and connect it to the 'red' rail in two different sections. If the meter reads 0V then both rails really are 'red'. If it reads the full DCC voltage (around 14V) then one rail is 'red' and the other 'black'. Swap the connections over in one of the sections and try again.

If you operate point motors and other accessories using DCC you may wish to have a separate booster and track bus for them to avoid their current draw affecting the trains. Another possibility is to use point motor decoders that have their own capacitor discharge unit (CDU) which will provide the large kick that solenoid point motors need to operate without leaving the rest of the layout short of power.

Regardless of the number of boosters or cut-outs that you have installed, you will find it really useful to add a number of switches along each track bus to turn off sections of track for troubleshooting purposes. It is far easier to locate a short circuit if you can work out roughly where it is. The track connected to each section of the bus will need to be isolated from the other track sections on both rails for the switches to work.

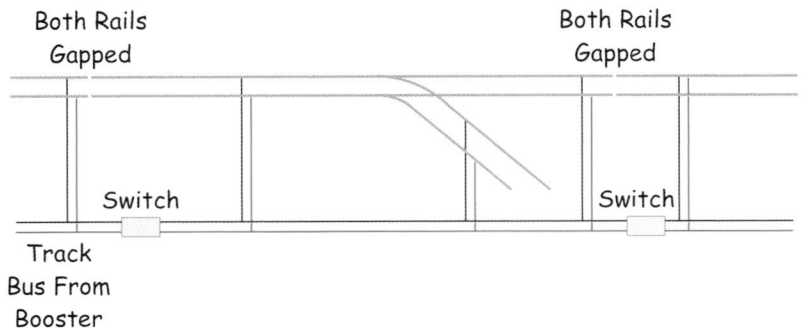

Both Rails Gapped

Both Rails Gapped

Switch

Switch

Track Bus From Booster

When trying to locate a short circuit you can turn the switches off one by one, working back towards the booster, until the short circuit clears. This tells you that the short circuit is in the section controlled by the last switch that you turned off. Using the diagram as an example, suppose that there is a locomotive causing a short circuit at the point. Turning off the right-hand switch would not clear the short. Turning off the left-hand switch would. From this you would know that the short was in the centre section of the track and could quickly home in on the problem.

Points and Crossings

Despite the many myths and misinformation to the contrary, there is no fundamental difference in wiring up points for DCC. The only thing to remember is that with DCC all rails that have power fed into them are always live whereas with analogue DC the power could be switched off.

The illustrations below all show live frog points. As with analogue DC, live frog points ensure electrical contact for the locomotive and make for smoother running. Peco Streamline 'electrofrog' points can be laid with no extra wiring. Most other brands require the frog and associated rails to be electrically switched when the point is changed. This can be done by a switch linked to the point motor or lever.

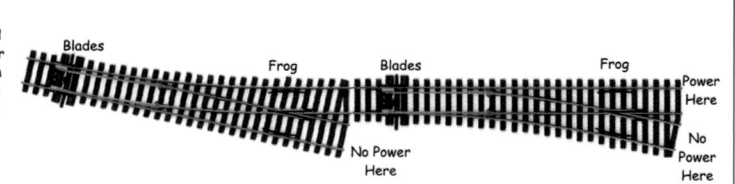

The secret with any pointwork is to always feed electrical power from the toe of the points. One feed can run through a number of points as long as they all face in the same direction, or to put it another way, when coming from the feed you should always pass the point blades before you get to the frog.

You will note that the turnouts retain their power switching function under DCC and that the sidings with the points set against them are electrically dead. This is an advantage if you are running unconverted locomotives on the layout as they can be isolated by setting the points against them. On the downside it means that any DCC equipped locomotive on the isolated siding will not respond to the controller.

To make a siding live at all times you need to put insulating rail joiners on both rails after the frog and then run feeder wires to the siding. The siding will now be live at all times but you will be able to run a locomotive into a point that is set against it and cause a short circuit which will shut down the booster. This is the single most common cause of short circuits on DCC layouts.

Don't forget that there can be a long length of track between any of the points and that they can fan out in both directions from the feed.

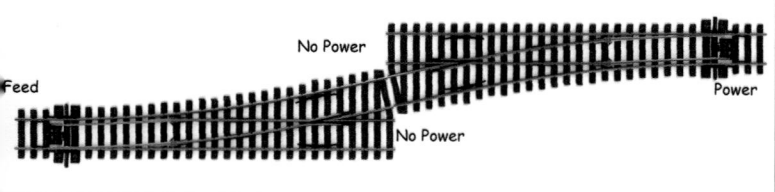

The situation to avoid is where you reach the frog before the blades. Whilst the power flows normally if the route through the points is set, things start to get complicated when you change the points.

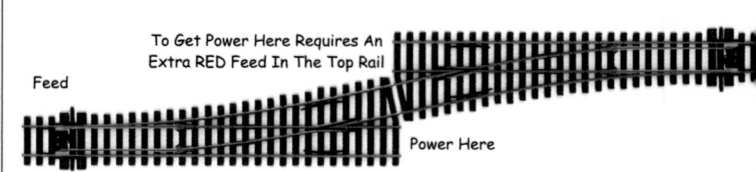

If the points are both set against each other then trains will still run on the lower line. To get a train to run on the upper line you will need to provide an extra power feed in the top rail, but note that it is the opposite polarity to the previous illustration.

And finally, if the points are set any other way you will get a short circuit that will cause your booster to shut down.

The solution is to put insulating rail joiners between the two points and feed each one from its toe. Don't forget that there can be many feet of track between the points and it can sometimes be hard to spot this track configuration.

The other problems that can occur with points is when out-of-gauge wheelsets bridge the gap between the frog rails and running rails to cause a short or where locomotives with long rigid wheelbases are running around sharp curves. If you must do this then the point needs to be modified so that the blades are connected to the adjacent running rail and the frog is electrically switched by the point motor or lever. The instructions supplied with Peco points explain how to do this.

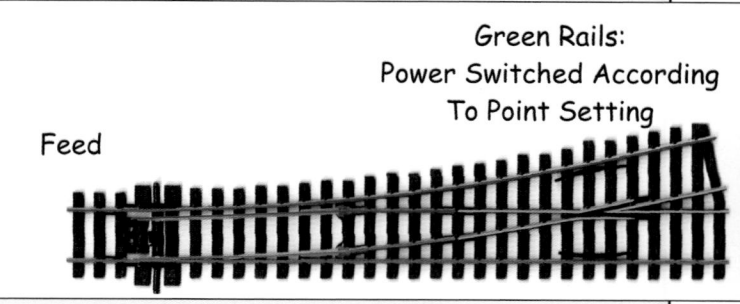

Reverse Loops and Wyes

Despite its many advanced capabilities, DCC is still a two-rail system and as such suffers from the same problems with reverse loops and wyes as analogue DC model railways.

The problem is that at some point the right-hand rail meets a left-hand rail and vice versa, resulting in an immediate short circuit.

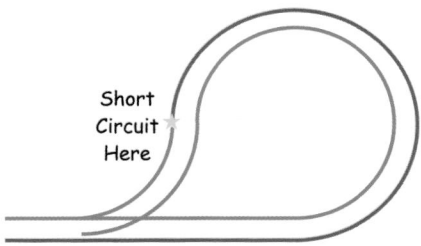

Short Circuit Here

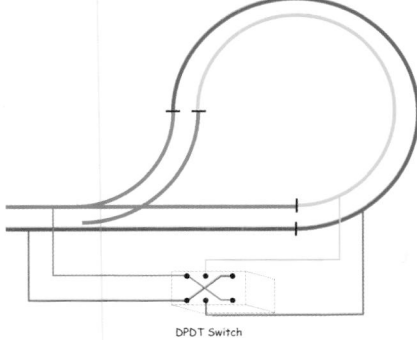

DPDT Switch

For conventional analogue systems the most common solution is to use a switch to change the polarity of either the loop or the rest of the layout. This is either operated manually or linked to a point. Assuming that the loop is fed through the switch the system is operated like this:

- Set the switch for the inbound direction
- Run the train onto the loop and stop
- Change the point and switch
- Run the train out of the loop (with the controller set to the opposite direction).

Fortunately you can use DCC in just the same way – with the exception that the train will still go forwards without having to change the direction on the controller.

Some manufacturers produce reverse loop modules which allow you to run a train around the loop without stopping or having to change a switch. These work by detecting the short circuit caused when the train enters or leaves the loop and quickly switching over the power feeds to the two rails. The decoder does not register the interruption in the power and continues running as before. These units cost upwards of £30.

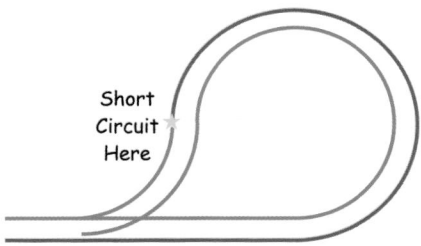

Reverse Loop Module

Whilst you could connect more than one reverse loop to them, they can cope with only one train at a time so in most situations you would need one for each reverse loop.

Wyes have exactly the same problem, and solution. Both reverse loops and wyes can hide in track plans that seem to be perfectly innocuous. It is always worth drawing out the track plan with both rails marked so that you can spot any problem areas.

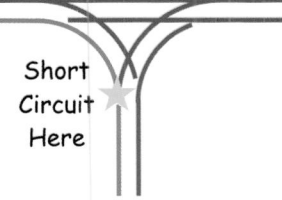

Short Circuit Here

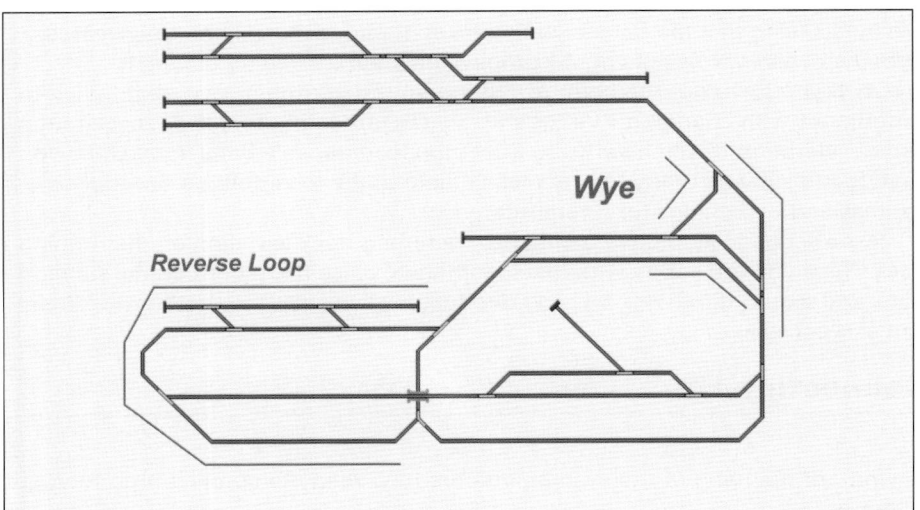

Reverse Loop

Wye

This track plan illustrates two problem areas with both DCC and analogue DC layouts: wyes and reverse loops.

CHAPTER

First Use

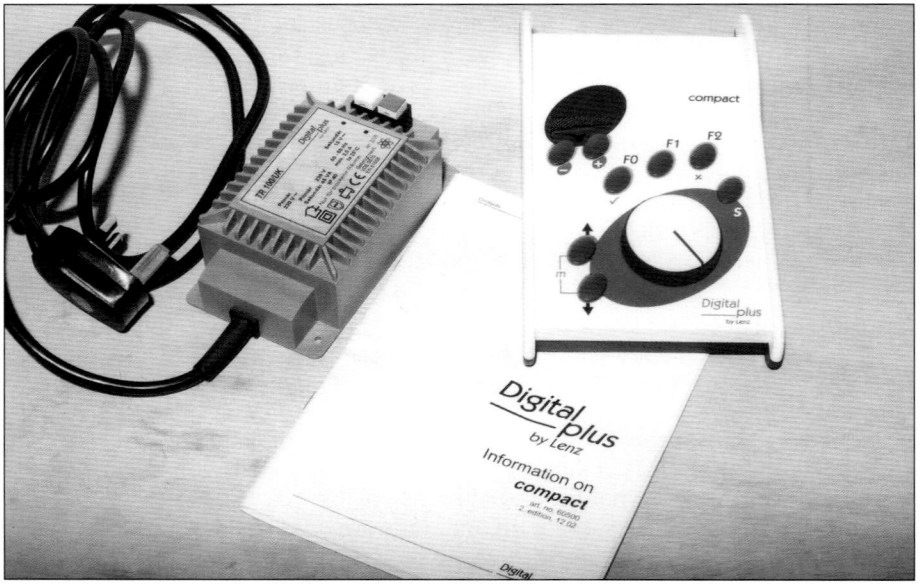

Once you have unpacked your DCC system you will be eager to use it, but it is vital that you take the time to read the instructions to avoid damaging either the unit or your locomotives.

This is it. You've unpacked your command station and fitted a decoder to a locomotive. Now you can't wait to get started. So what should you do first?

Read the instructions. I know it sounds terribly dull but virtually all command station manuals include a 'quick start' or similar section that will give you enough information to set the system up and run a train without getting too frustrated or damaging anything.

Don't get carried away and start wiring your unit straight into your layout. The first thing to do is set up a section of programming track so that you can check your first locomotive conversion(s).

Following the instructions, connect the various components together and connect the programming track outputs to a length of track. Turn the power on and check that the command station and cab show the correct lights and displays.

Take your first DCC converted locomotive and place it on the programming track. Following the instructions for your particular DCC system, check that the decoder responds correctly. You can now set the locomotive address.

Now connect a second length of track, or ideally an oval, to the track terminals of your booster unit. Check that the track wiring is OK by placing a coin across the rails and seeing that the booster shuts down. Remove the coin and, if necessary, reset the booster. Now put your locomotive on the track and try driving it.

Once you have got the hang of driving your locomotive you might wish to experiment with changing CVs for start voltage, maximum speed, acceleration and deceleration to see how these affect the locomotive's behaviour. Once you have found settings that you like, make a note of the locomotive's decoder type, address and CV settings for future reference.

Test a second locomotive on the programming track and then on the running track. Once you are happy with that locomotive, place them both on the running track and experiment with running two locomotives at once, both individually and as a consist.

Connecting Up

Having got the hang of the system, you are now ready to connect it up to your layout.

Running Analogue Locomotives with DCC

Most DCC systems allow you to run a standard analogue locomotive on your DCC system. Whilst this is very useful you should be aware that analogue locomotives should not be left standing on powered track for more than a few minutes at a time.

Any analogue locomotive left standing on a DCC powered track will seem to buzz. This is due to the track voltage continuously changing between a positive voltage of around 14V to a negative one, and back again. Whilst the average voltage seen by the motor is zero and thus the motor doesn't run, the constant changes of voltage do cause the motor to buzz and heat up. If the locomotive is left in this state for more than a few minutes the heat can cause the motor windings to melt and the motor to expire with a wisp of smoke. To avoid this you need to ensure that any analogue locomotive

that is not in motion or temporarily stopped is either removed from the layout or parked on an isolated track.

To run analogue locomotives the DCC system stretches some of the pulses, either on the positive or negative cycle, depending on the direction of travel required. This changes the overall average voltage seen by the locomotive, whilst not affecting DCC operation. This means that the DC voltage seen by an analogue locomotive is pulsed rather than smooth DC. Whilst this can give better slow speed performance from some locomotives, the rapid pulsing will destroy high-quality coreless motors, such as the Escap range. These are normally found only in kit-built locomotives, but if you are in any doubt DO NOT run an analogue locomotive on DCC until you have checked that it is not fitted with a coreless motor.

Assuming that you are replacing one or more analogue controllers your first task is to disconnect all the controllers. If you have a cab control system, where any controller can connect to any track section, you need to set all the cab switches to the same cab and connect the DCC system in place of that controller. If each of your analogue controllers is connected to a specific track section then you will need to connect the DCC system in place of all the controllers. Either way, don't forget to turn on any isolating sections used for holding locomotives.

Wire up the DCC command station/booster following the instructions and double-check your connections before you turn on the power.

Test that a short circuit on the track will cause the system to shut down by placing a screwdriver or coin across the track with the DCC system on. If the system does not shut down immediately you will need to improve your wiring – see Chapter 6 Wiring for DCC.

Place a locomotive fitted with a decoder on the track, set its address on the controller and start driving.

If you encounter problems then consult the troubleshooting guide at the end of this book or the equivalent section in your command station manual.

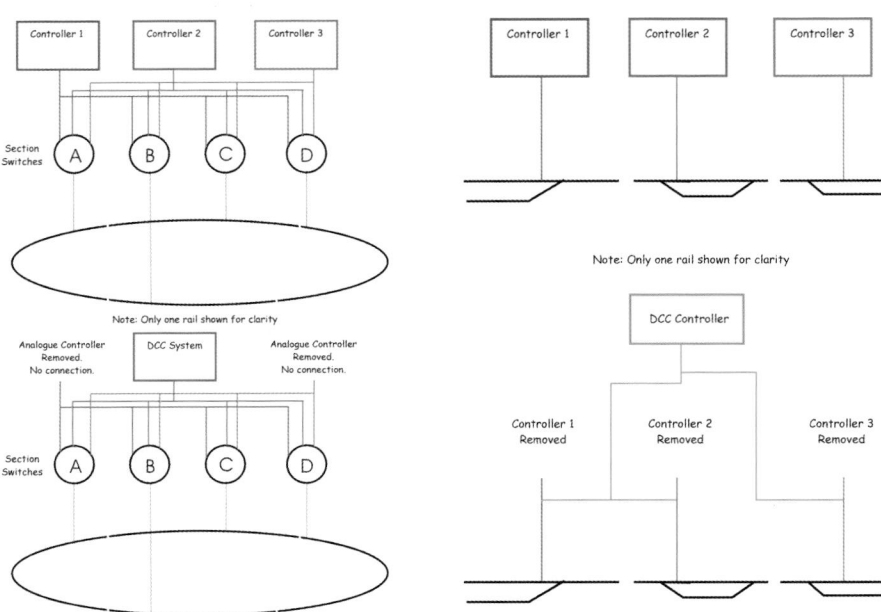

Connecting a DCC system to a layout in place of an existing cab control system.

Connecting a DCC system to a layout in place of individual controllers.

One common problem is a short circuit caused by running up to a point that is set against the locomotive. The solution is not to do it – real engine drivers don't, so neither should you.

Programming Tracks

It is useful to have a programming track on your layout, but you will probably want it connected to the rest of the trackage so that you don't have to lift locomotives off the rails to change their CV settings. Even if your DCC system allows you to program 'on the main' you will find that in order to read the settings you will still need to use the programming track. If you have a simple system, such as the Bachmann E-Z controller, that does not have a separate programming track output, it is still useful to create a programming track to save you having to take all the other locomotives off the layout every time that you want to set a locomotive's address.

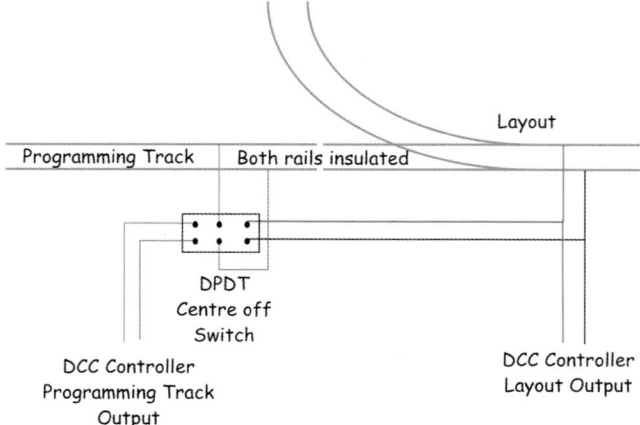

The diagram above shows how to convert a siding on your layout into a programming track using the programming track outputs from your DCC system. It is important that the DPDT switch is a centre-off type so that there is no possibility of the programming and normal outputs of the controller being connected to the programming track at the same time. Both rails need to be electrically isolated from the main layout using insulated rail joiners.

In normal use the switch would be set to connect the siding to the layout and it would behave just like any other siding. To program a locomotive you need to drive it onto the siding. Make sure that the whole locomotive is in the siding and no wheels are on the layout side of the insulated gap. Change the switch to connect the siding to the programming output of the controller. You can now program the decoder. Once you have finished, change the switch to connect the siding back to the layout and drive the locomotive off the siding.

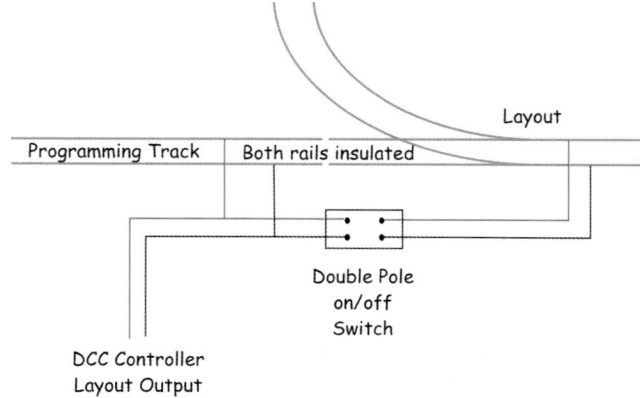

The diagram at the bottom of page 60 shows how to convert a siding on your layout into a programming track for a simple system, such as the Bachmann E-Z controller, that does not have programming track outputs. The programming track will not add any extra functions to the controller but will enable you to change decoder addresses without having to remove locomotives from the layout. In this case the switch is a double pole on/off switch.

In normal use the switch would be 'ON' so that power is fed to both the siding and the layout. To change a locomotive's address you need to drive it onto the siding. Make sure that the whole locomotive is in the siding and no wheels are on the layout side of the insulated gap. Change the switch to 'OFF'. The siding will still have power but the rest of the layout will no longer be connected to the DCC system. You can now change the locomotive's address. Once you have finished, change the switch back to 'ON' and drive the locomotive off the siding.

Three suggested suppliers of suitable switches are listed below:

DPDT centre-off:

Maplin Electronics Ltd.	part no.	FH05F Sub-min Toggle F
Rapid Electronics Ltd.	part no.	75-0145 DPDT Centre-off
Squires Model & Craft Tools	part no.	MT0080 Mini Toggle DPDT C/Off On-Off-On

DPDT on/off

Maplin Electronics Ltd.	part no.	FH04E Sub-min Toggle E
Rapid Electronics Ltd.	part no.	75-0140 DPDT
Squires Model & Craft Tools	part no.	MT0070 Mini Toggle DPDT On-On

Double-heading is always a favourite with enthusiasts and is necessary for a number of operational reasons. This photo shows Nos 45353 and 73134 passing Salford on a heavily-loaded passenger working from Manchester Exchange to Llandudno Junction in the summer of 1963. Author's collection

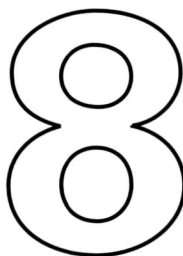

CHAPTER

Configuring Locomotive Decoders

All sorts of information which controls the way that a locomotive will perform is held in the Configuration Variables (CV) in the decoder. These can be set to suit your needs.

Not all CVs are implemented in all decoders. Basic decoders will have only limited functionality. The CVs that should be available in all decoders are indicated by an M in the Status column of the table below.

The NMRA recommend that a number of CVs are implemented in all decoders but they are not mandatory. These are indicated by an R in the Status column. All other CVs are optional and are indicated by an O.

Not all the available CVs have been allocated a purpose. The NMRA have reserved some for future expansion of the standards whilst others are reserved for manufacturer's own specific functions. Thus some of your decoders may have features using CVs that are not listed in the table.

CV Number	Status	Description	Default	CV Number	Status	Description	Default
1	M	Primary Locomotive Address	3	24	O	Braking Adjustment	
2	R	Start Voltage	0	25	O	Speed Table	
3	R	Acceleration Rate	0	26	O	Not Currently Used	
4	R	Braking Rate	0	27	O	Automatic Stopping	
5	O	Top Speed	255	28	O	Bi-directional Communication	
6	O	Speed Curve Modifier	0	29	M	Basic Configuration Register	n/a
7	M	Manufacturer Version Number	n/a	30	O	Error Information	n/a
8	M	Manufacturer ID Number	n/a	31	O	Decoder Sub-address	
9	O	Total PWM Period	n/a	32	O	Decoder Sub-address Flag	
10	O	EMF Feedback Cut-out	0	33-46	O	Function Output Locations	
11	R	Packet Time-out		47-64	O	Not Currently Used	
12	O	Power Source Conversion		65	O	Kick Start	
13-14	O	Alternate Mode Function Status		66	O	Forward Trim	
15-16	O	Not Currently Used		67-94	O	Special Speed Table	
17-18	O	Extended Address		95	O	Reverse Trim	
19	O	Consist Address		96-104	O	Not Currently Used	
20	O	Not Currently Used		105-6	O	User Identification	
21-22	O	Consist Address Active for Functions		107-11	O	Not Currently Used	
23	O	Acceleration Adjustment		112-28	O	Use Specified By Manufacturers	

CV 1 Primary Locomotive Address
As supplied, all decoders have CV 1 set to 3. This means that the decoder will respond to loco number 3. To change the locomotive's address, you change the value of CV 1 to a number between 1 and 127. If the decoder and your base station support extended addressing then the numbers 128 through to 9999 can be used – but there is a special method to do this.

CV 2 Start Voltage
This sets the voltage that will correspond to the first speed step. Decoders vary as to how the value is interpreted so you should check the instructions, but the normal range is 0 to 255. This value should be set as low as possible to just keep the locomotive moving. In a perfect world it would be set to zero, but the friction of the locomotive's mechanism mean that the optimum value will be larger than that. The correct figure is best established by experimentation and could well be different for apparently identical locomotives. A high figure, over 70, would indicate that the locomotive mechanism could do with some remedial attention.

CV 3 Acceleration Rate

This determines how quickly the locomotive will accelerate. Large freight locomotives will normally take longer to reach a given speed than an express locomotive and this enables you to replicate these differences. Many analogue controllers have similar features, usually labelled 'momentum'.

The rate of acceleration is worked out as CV 3 x 0.896 / Number of speed steps seconds per speed step.

For example:

CV 3 = 2 and number of speed steps = 128 then the acceleration rate is 2 x 0.896 / 128 = 0.014 seconds per step. So to accelerate from 0 to half speed (64 steps) would take 64 x 0.014 = 0.896 seconds.

Or:

CV 3 = 100 and number of speed steps = 28 then the acceleration rate is 100 x 0.896 / 28 = 3.2 seconds per step. So to accelerate from 0 to quarter speed (7 steps) would take 7 x 3.2 = 22.4 seconds.

If CV 3 is set to zero then the change in speed is immediate.

CV 4 Braking Rate

This determines how quickly the locomotive will decelerate. It works in exactly the same way as CV 3 Acceleration Rate (above) but can have a different value. It normally takes longer to stop a train than to get it going.

CV 5 Top Speed

This is used to limit the top speed of the locomotive. Most model locomotives can go much faster than the real thing. By setting CV 5 so that the locomotive is travelling at a slower top speed you not only make operations more realistic but enable the speed steps to have more effect.

The default value is the maximum of 255 and allows the full voltage to reach the motor. Decreasing this value reduces the maximum voltage reaching the motor. For OO gauge the DCC track power is normally 14 to 16 volts. Once this has been converted from AC to DC by the decoder the maximum voltage available to the motor will be in the region of 11 to 13 volts. Typically for every 10 you subtract from CV 5 you will reduce the maximum voltage by about 0.5V.

CV 6 Speed Curve Modifier

This is used to set the motor voltage at the middle of the range of speed steps. This allows you to tailor the voltage output to suit the locomotive's motor. Setting a low value means that the low speed steps will be closely spaced, whilst the high ones are farther apart. Setting a high value has the opposite effect. The combination of CV 2 (Start Voltage), CV 5 (Top Speed) and CV 6 gives great flexibility in determining how a locomotive will respond to the range of speed steps.

The default value of 0 indicates that the Speed Curve Modifier is not being used. Setting it to the mid-range value of 128 will have the same effect.

For OO gauge decoders the motor voltage at the middle speed step is typically 6V. For every 10 that you add or subtract from 128 you will increase or decrease the mid-point voltage by about 0.5V.

CV 7 Manufacturer Version Number

You cannot change this value. It is set by the manufacturer and indicates the version of the decoder that you have. It has no effect on the performance of the locomotive.

CV 8 Manufacturer ID Number

You cannot change this value. It is set by the manufacturer and indicates the identification number issued to the manufacturer by the NMRA. It has no effect on the performance of the locomotive.

CV 9 Total PWM Period

If the decoder uses pulse width modulation (PWM) for the motor output then this CV sets the length of the pulses. If your decoder uses PWM then you should consult the decoder's documentation to establish suitable settings. A value of 0 indicates that PWM is either not available on the decoder or is not in use.

CV 10 EMF Feedback Cut-out

If the decoder uses back-EMF to regulate the motor speed then this CV allows you to set the speed step above which it is no longer used. Back-EMF is a way of measuring how fast a motor is running. This can be used to establish if the motor needs more or less voltage to maintain the desired speed. This ensures that trains do not slow down when climbing hills, or run away when descending them. It is also of great help in getting motors to run slowly for shunting operations. Many analogue controllers have similar features usually labelled 'feedback'. A value of 0 indicates that EMF feedback is either not available on the decoder or is not being used.

CV 11 Packet Timeout

Gives the maximum period of time that the decoder will maintain its current speed without receiving a valid message from the command station.

CV 12 Power Source Conversion

Defines how the locomotive is powered if the decoder address (CV 1) is set to zero. This is chiefly provided for compatibility with older command control systems such as Hornby's Zero-1 and you are unlikely to need to amend it.

CV 13 Alternate Mode Function Status

Defines which functions (F1 – F8) can be controlled if the decoder is operating on a different command control system (as set by CV 12). You are unlikely to need to amend this value.

CV 14 Alternate Mode Function 2 Status

Defines which functions (F9 – F12 and FL) can be controlled if the decoder is operating on a different command control system (as set by CV 12). You are unlikely to need to amend this value.

CV 17/18 Extended Address

When a locomotive decoder is set up to use extended (4 digit) addressing these two variables contain the address. (To establish if extended addressing is in use you need to check bit 5 of CV 29). CV 17 is the first byte of the address and CV 18 the second. CV 17 must have a binary value between 11000000 and 11100111 inclusive to be valid.

CV 19 Consist Address

Where the locomotive is in a consist this CV indicates the consist's address. Bit 7 indicates the relative direction within the consist (0 indicates normal operation, 1 indicates that the locomotive is in reverse when the consist is moving forwards). Bits 6 to 0 indicate the consist's address. A value of zero indicates that the unit is not part of a consist.

CV 21 Consist Address Active for F1 – F8

Where the locomotive is in a consist this CV defines if functions F1 through to F8 will respond to instructions sent to both the locomotive and the consist, or just the locomotive. Each bit is used to control a function. A value of 0 indicates that the function will respond only to instructions sent to the locomotive's address. A value of 1 indicates that the function will respond to instructions sent to both the locomotive's and consist's addresses. F1 is controlled by bit 0, F2 by bit 1, F3 by bit 4 and so on up to F8 which is controlled by bit 7. Using CV 21 and 22 enables you to select which functions are applied to the consist as a whole or individual locomotives within it, such as headlights on the front locomotive and tail lights on the rear one.

CV 22 Consist Address Active for F9 – F12 and FL

Where the locomotive is in a consist this CV defines if functions F9 through to F12 and FL will respond to instructions sent to both the locomotive and the consist, or just the locomotive. Each bit is used to control a function. A value of 0 indicates that the function will respond only to instructions sent to the locomotive's address. A value of 1 indicates that the function will respond to instructions sent to both the locomotive's and consist's addresses. FL in the forward direction is controlled by bit 0, FL in reverse by bit 1, F9 by bit 4 and so on up to F12 which is controlled by bit 5.

CV 23 Acceleration Adjustment

This value affects the normal acceleration rate for the locomotive set in CV 3 Acceleration Rate. The intended use is to enable you to change the momentum of the train to simulate differing loads whilst retaining the normal value unchanged. Thus the adjustment could be 0 for a light engine and 100 for a long mineral train.

The value can range from 0 to 127 with the adjustment being either positive or negative. The adjusted acceleration rate is calculated as: CV 23 x 0.896 / Number of speed steps in use.

CV 24 Braking Adjustment

This value affects the normal deceleration rate for the locomotive set in CV 4 Braking Rate. The intended use is to enable you to change the momentum of the train to simulate differing loads whilst retaining the normal value unchanged. Thus the adjustment could be 0 for a light engine and 100 for a long mineral train.

The value can range from 0 to 127 with the adjustment being either positive or negative. The adjusted braking rate is calculated as: CV 24 x 0.896 / Number of speed steps in use.

CV 25 Speed Table / Mid-range Speed Step

This value is used either to indicate which preset speed table is to be used or the particular speed step that will produce the mid-range motor speed.

A value of 0 or 1 indicates that the CV is not being used or is not available on the decoder.

A value of 2 indicates a linear curve. The motor speed will increase by an equal amount for each speed step.

A value between 3 and 127 indicates which of the built-in speed tables will be used.

A value between 128 and 153 defines which of the 28 speed steps will make the motor run at half-speed. 128 is equivalent to step 1, 129 to step 2, 130 to step 3, through to 153 for position 26. It is not possible to set the mid-range speed step to steps 0 or 27. If the decoder operates with 14 speed steps then the value will be divided by two.

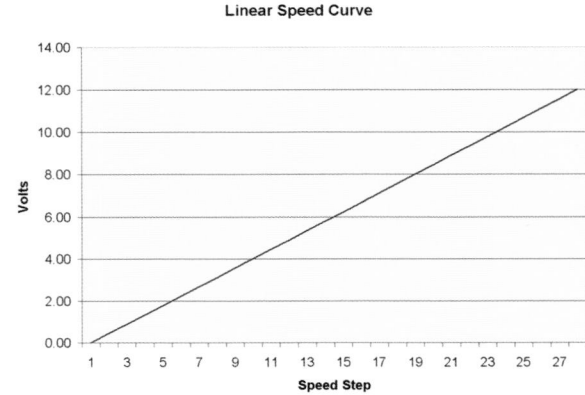

CV 27 Automatic Stopping Configuration

This CV is under re-evaluation by the NMRA and may be amended. It is used to define the conditions that will cause the decoder to automatically stop the locomotive.

Bit 0 Enable/disable automatic stopping in the presence of an asymmetrical DCC signal which is more positive on the right rail (when facing forwards). A value of 0 indicates disabled or that the function is not available on the decoder; a value of 1 that it is enabled.

Bit 1 Enable/disable automatic stopping in the presence of an asymmetrical DCC signal which is more positive on the left rail (when facing forwards). A value of 0 indicates disabled or that the function is not available on the decoder; a value of 1 that it is enabled.

An asymmetrical DCC signal is one that reaches a higher positive voltage than negative, or vice versa. It is used to create sections of track that automatically slow a train to a halt, for example in front of signals or on dead end sidings. See Chapter 9 Advanced Use for more details.

Bit 2 Enable/disable automatic stopping in the presence of a signal controlled cut-out signal. A value of 0 indicates disabled or that the function is not available on the decoder, a value of 1 that it is enabled. This is a special DCC signal that tells all locomotives that receive it to slow to a stop. Like asymmetrical DCC signals, it is normally used to stop trains overrunning red signals.

Bit 3 Not currently used.

Bit 4 Enable/disable automatic stopping in the presence of forward polarity DC. A value of 0 indicates disabled or that the function is not available on the decoder; a value of 1 that it is enabled. This is used to override the decoder's normal behaviour if it finds itself on a DC powered track section. Normally if the DC voltage would cause the locomotive to move forwards it will adjust its speed to match the DC voltage. If this bit is set to 1 then instead of changing speed the locomotive will stop.

Bits 6 and 7 Not currently used.

CV 28 Bi-directional Communication Configuration

This CV is under re-evaluation by the NMRA and may be amended. It is used to define the way that the decoder handles bi-directional communications. For more details of bi-directional communications see Chapter 9 Advanced Use.

Bit 0 Enable/disable unsolicited decoder initiated transmissions. A value of 0 indicates disabled or that the function is not available on the decoder; a value of 1 that it is enabled. Setting the value to 1 indicates that the decoder can start communications rather than waiting for something to ask it for information.

Bit 1 Enable/disable initiated broadcast transmissions using asymmetrical DCC signal. A value of 0 indicates disabled or that the function is not available on the decoder; a value of 1 that it is enabled.

Bit 2 Enable/disable initiated broadcast transmissions using a signal controlled signal. A value of 0 indicates disabled or that the function is not available on the decoder; a value of 1 that it is enabled.

Bits 3, 4, 5, 6 and 7 Not currently used.

CV 29 Basic Configuration Register

This variable contains a number of different settings that do not justify their own unique CV.

Bit 0 Direction Of Travel

Set to 0 = Normal. Locomotive moves forward when controller is set to forward.

Set to 1 = Reversed. Locomotive has either been wired incorrectly or it is wished to operate this locomotive in reverse. For example the 'tail' locomotive of a pair of BR Class 20 diesels.

Bit 1 Speed Steps

Set to 0 = Operates with 14 or 27 speed steps. Used when the decoder can support 28/128 steps but the command station cannot.

Set to 1 = Operates with 28 or 128 speed steps.

Bit 2 Analogue Mode
Set to 0 = Locomotive will respond only to DCC signals. It will not operate on analogue layouts.
Set to 1 = Locomotive can be operated on both DC and analogue layouts.

Bit 3 Bi-directional Communications
Set to '0' if bi-directional communications are not in use or the decoder is not designed to use them.
Set to '1' if bi-directional communications are in use.

Bit 4 Speed Table
Set to 0 = Uses default speed table (set in CV 2 and CV 5).
Set to 1 = Uses special speed table set in CV 66 to 95.

Bit 5 Address System
Set to 0 = Uses base address (set in CV 1).
Set to 1 = Uses extended address (set in CV 17 and CV 18).

Bit 6 No current use.

Bit 7 Decoder type.
Set to '0' for multi-function decoder (motor and function outputs).
Set to '1' for accessory decoder (no motor control).

To set or decode the values see the notes on Binary/Hex Conversion on page 69.

CV 30 Error Information

You cannot change this value. It is set by the decoder if there is a problem or error. Apart from a zero value indicating 'no error' the values are specified by the decoder manufacturer. Refer to the decoder's documentation to establish what any codes mean. It has no effect on the performance of the locomotive.

CV 31 Decoder Sub-address

This CV is under re-evaluation by the NMRA and may be amended. It is used to differentiate different decoders in the same locomotive or multiple unit. For example, you might have a decoder in each car of a multiple unit to control lighting, or you might have two decoders in a locomotive to provide extra function outputs. Each decoder will respond to the same locomotive address. The sub-address is used when the settings on a particular decoder need to be changed in isolation from the other decoders.

Bits 0-3 contain the decoder's sub-address. If the value is 0 then the decoder has no sub-address. The maximum number of decoders that can be operated individually on one address using sub-addresses is 7.

Bits 4-7 Not currently used.

CV 32 Decoder Sub-address Flag

This CV is under re-evaluation by the NMRA and may be amended. It is used to indicate which of the sub-decoders respond to queries from other DCC accessories.

Bit 0 Used to designate the decoder which will respond to bi-directional communication requests. If the value is 1 then the decoder will process bi-directional communications. If the value is set to 0 it will not. Only one decoder in the locomotive or multiple unit should have this bit set to 1.

Bit 1 Used to designate the decoder which will respond to long form CV access instructions. If the value is set to 1 then the decoder will respond to these instructions, if the value is set to 0 it will not. Only one decoder in the locomotive or multiple unit should have this bit set to 1.

Bits 2-7 Not currently used?

CV 33-46 Function Output Locations

These CVs allow you to allocate which function on your cab controls a specific function output on the decoder. This enables you to reallocate the function outputs to suit your installation. For example, if you have installed two four function decoders in a locomotive you could specify that decoder 1's outputs responded to FL(f) (forward lights), F1, F12 and F2 while decoder 2's outputs responded to FL(r) (reverse lights), F3, F11 and F2. In addition you can make a single function key control more than one function output on the decoder, useful if you need to operate something that draws too high a current for a single output.

Each CV configures a different function. The CV value indicates which outputs the function will control. Each bit corresponds to one potential output.

Bit 0 – FL(f), Bit 1 – FL(r), Bit 2 – F1, Bit 3 – F2 and so on up to Bit 14 – F12. Bits 15 and 16 are not used.

CV	Function	Default Value
CV 33	FL(f) Forward headlight	0000000000000001
CV 34	FL(r) Reverse headlight	0000000000000010
CV 35	F1	0000000000000100
CV 36	F2	0000000000001000
CV 37	F3	0000000000010000
CV 38	F4	0000000000100000
CV 39	F5	0000000001000000
CV 40	F6	0000000010000000
CV 41	F7	0000000100000000
CV 42	F8	0000001000000000
CV 43	F9	0000010000000000
CV 44	F10	0000100000000000
CV 45	F11	0001000000000000
CV 46	F12	0010000000000000

So to change the normal F1 output on a decoder to respond to F5 you would need to make the following changes:

> CV 35 F1 key – change from the default value of 0000000000000100 (operates F1 output) to 0000000000000000 (operates no output)
>
> CV 39 F5 key – change from the default value of 0000000001000000 (operates F5 output) to 0000000000000100 (operates F1 output).

To change a decoder so that the F1 and F2 outputs both responded to the F1 key you would need to make the following changes:

> CV 35 F1 key – change from the default value of 0000000000000100 (operates F1 output) to 0000000000001100 (operates F2 and F1 outputs).
>
> CV 36 F2 key – change from the default value of 0000000000001000 (operates F2 output) to 0000000000000000 (operates no output)

CV 65 Kick Start

Specifies the extra voltage 'kick' that will be supplied to the motor when moving from stop to the first speed step. This is used to overcome the mechanical resistance that many older motors have when starting to turn. The extra voltage jolts them into motion and is then removed so that they run at the specified speed.

CV 66 Forward Trim

Specifies a factor to be applied to the voltage level when the locomotive is moving forwards. This is used to make the locomotive travel faster (or slower) when going forwards than it would normally for any given speed step. If the value is 0 then no forward trim is applied. For values between 1 and 255 the adjustment is calculated as Normal Speed x (CV 66 / 128). So a value of 128 would cause the forward and normal speeds to be the same. A value less than 128 would cause the forward speed to be less than the normal speed and a value greater than 128 would cause the forward speed to be greater than the normal speed.

This CV is of great use when running locomotives double-headed as it allows you to adjust their individual speeds to match without having to overwrite the normal decoder settings.

CV 67-94 Special Speed Table

Allows you to tailor the speed of the locomotive at each speed step to suit your requirements. As not all motors perform in the same way you can use the speed table to make them perform consistently. Some motors require larger changes in voltage at slow speeds. By changing the output for each speed step you can optimise each decoder's performance to suit the motor to which it is connected.

CV 95 Reverse Trim

Specifies a factor to be applied to the voltage level when the locomotive is moving backwards. This is used to make the locomotive travel faster (or slower) when going backwards than it would normally for any given speed step. If the value is 0 then no reverse trim is applied. For values between 1 and 255 the adjustment is calculated as Normal Speed x (CV 95 / 128). So a value of 128 would cause the backward and normal speeds to be the same. A value less than 128 would cause the backward speed to be less than the normal speed and a value greater than 128 would cause the backward speed to be greater than the normal speed.

This CV is of great use when running locomotives double-headed as it allows you to adjust their individual speeds to match without having to overwrite the normal decoder settings.

CV 105 & 106 User Identification

These CVs are reserved for the locomotive's owner to store identification information. In the US the recommendation is to use your NMRA membership number. There is no equivalent in the UK, but selecting a random value to use for all your locomotives might enable you to prove ownership if that was ever necessary.

Binary/Hexadecimal/Decimal Conversion

Where a number of variables are combined in one CV the DCC system uses a binary number system. Depending on which system you use, you may need to enter the values as binary, hexadecimal or decimal numbers.

Binary Entry

This is simply the value (1 or 0) for each value in turn, starting from bit 7 and running to bit 0.

For example, suppose you wish to enter the following setting:
Bit 0 = 0, Bit 1 = 1, Bit 2 = 1, Bit 3 = 0, Bit 4 = 0, Bit 5 = 0, Bit 6 = 0, Bit 7 = 0.
First you would reverse the order:
Bit 7 = 0, Bit 6 = 0, Bit 5 = 0, Bit 4 = 0, Bit 3 = 0, Bit 2 = 1, Bit 1 = 1, Bit 0 = 0.
Then you would enter 00000110 on the keypad.

Hexadecimal Entry

Some systems require the binary entry to be converted to hexadecimal. This is a number system based on 0-15 instead of 0-9.

An 8 bit binary number converts to two hexadecimal digits.

Binary	Hexadecimal	Binary	Hexadecimal	Binary	Hexadecimal	Binary	Hexadecimal
0000	0	1000	8	0100	4	1100	C
0001	1	1001	9	0101	5	1101	D
0010	2	1010	A	0110	6	1110	E
0011	3	1011	B	0111	7	1111	F

Thus our binary number of 0000 0110 would be entered as 06.
A binary number of 1101 0011 would be entered as D3.

Decimal Entry

Some systems require a decimal entry. In this case the eight digit binary number converts to a number between 0 and 255.

The value can be calculated as follows:
Bit 7 x 128 + Bit 6 x 64 + Bit 5 x 32 + Bit 4 x 16 + Bit 3 x 8 + Bit 2 x 4 + Bit 1 x 2 + Bit 0.
The final value will never be greater than 255.

Using our binary number of 00000110 we would calculate:
128 x 0 + 64 x 0 + 32 x 0 + 16 x 0 + 8 x 0 + 4 x 1 + 2 x 1 + 0 = 6

So the value would be entered as 6.

As you can see from the table below, it is very important to know which type of number your system wants as '10' is very different in binary, hexadecimal and decimal. The table makes a very handy conversion tool from one number system to another.

Binary	Hexadecimal	Decimal	Binary	Hexadecimal	Decimal	Binary	Hexadecimal	Decimal
00000000	00	0	00100011	23	35	01000110	46	70
00000001	01	1	00100100	24	36	01000111	47	71
00000010	02	2	00100101	25	37	01001000	48	72
00000011	03	3	00100110	26	38	01001001	49	73
00000100	04	4	00100111	27	39	01001010	4A	74
00000101	05	5	00101000	28	40	01001011	4B	75
00000110	06	6	00101001	29	41	01001100	4C	76
00000111	07	7	00101010	2A	42	01001101	4D	77
00001000	08	8	00101011	2B	43	01001110	4E	78
00001001	09	9	00101100	2C	44	01001111	4F	79
00001010	0A	10	00101101	2D	45	01010000	50	80
00001011	0B	11	00101110	2E	46	01010001	51	81
00001100	0C	12	00101111	2F	47	01010010	52	82
00001101	0D	13	00110000	30	48	01010011	53	83
00001110	0E	14	00110001	31	49	01010100	54	84
00001111	0F	15	00110010	32	50	01010101	55	85
00010000	10	16	00110011	33	51	01010110	56	86
00010001	11	17	00110100	34	52	01010111	57	87
00010010	12	18	00110101	35	53	01011000	58	88
00010011	13	19	00110110	36	54	01011001	59	89
00010100	14	20	00110111	37	55	01011010	5A	90
00010101	15	21	00111000	38	56	01011011	5B	91
00010110	16	22	00111001	39	57	01011100	5C	92
00010111	17	23	00111010	3A	58	01011101	5D	93
00011000	18	24	00111011	3B	59	01011110	5E	94
00011001	19	25	00111100	3C	60	01011111	5F	95
00011010	1A	26	00111101	3D	61	01100000	60	96
00011011	1B	27	00111110	3E	62	01100001	61	97
00011100	1C	28	00111111	3F	63	01100010	62	98
00011101	1D	29	01000000	40	64	01100011	63	99
00011110	1E	30	01000001	41	65	01100100	64	100
00011111	1F	31	01000010	42	66	01100101	65	101
00100000	20	32	01000011	43	67	01100110	66	102
00100001	21	33	01000100	44	68	01100111	67	103
00100010	22	34	01000101	45	69	01101000	68	104

Binary	Hexadecimal	Decimal	Binary	Hexadecimal	Decimal	Binary	Hexadecimal	Decimal
01101001	69	105	10011100	9C	156	11001111	CF	207
01101010	6A	106	10011101	9D	157	11010000	D0	208
01101011	6B	107	10011110	9E	158	11010001	D1	209
01101100	6C	108	10011111	9F	159	11010010	D2	210
01101101	6D	109	10100000	A0	160	11010011	D3	211
01101110	6E	110	10100001	A1	161	11010100	D4	212
01101111	6F	111	10100010	A2	162	11010101	D5	213
01110000	70	112	10100011	A3	163	11010110	D6	214
01110001	71	113	10100100	A4	164	11010111	D7	215
01110010	72	114	10100101	A5	165	11011000	D8	216
01110011	73	115	10100110	A6	166	11011001	D9	217
01110100	74	116	10100111	A7	167	11011010	DA	218
01110101	75	117	10101000	A8	168	11011011	DB	219
01110110	76	118	10101001	A9	169	11011100	DC	220
01110111	77	119	10101010	AA	170	11011101	DD	221
01111000	78	120	10101011	AB	171	11011110	DE	222
01111001	79	121	10101100	AC	172	11011111	DF	223
01111010	7A	122	10101101	AD	173	11100000	E0	224
01111011	7B	123	10101110	AE	174	11100001	E1	225
01111100	7C	124	10101111	AF	175	11100010	E2	226
01111101	7D	125	10110000	B0	176	11100011	E3	227
01111110	7E	126	10110001	B1	177	11100100	E4	228
01111111	7F	127	10110010	B2	178	11100101	E5	229
10000000	80	128	10110011	B3	179	11100110	E6	230
10000001	81	129	10110100	B4	180	11100111	E7	231
10000010	82	130	10110101	B5	181	11101000	E8	232
10000011	83	131	10110110	B6	182	11101001	E9	233
10000100	84	132	10110111	B7	183	11101010	EA	234
10000101	85	133	10111000	B8	184	11101011	EB	235
10000110	86	134	10111001	B9	185	11101100	EC	236
10000111	87	135	10111010	BA	186	11101101	ED	237
10001000	88	136	10111011	BB	187	11101110	EE	238
10001001	89	137	10111100	BC	188	11101111	EF	239
10001010	8A	138	10111101	BD	189	11110000	F0	240
10001011	8B	139	10111110	BE	190	11110001	F1	241
10001100	8C	140	10111111	BF	191	11110010	F2	242
10001101	8D	141	11000000	C0	192	11110011	F3	243
10001110	8E	142	11000001	C1	193	11110100	F4	244
10001111	8F	143	11000010	C2	194	11110101	F5	245
10010000	90	144	11000011	C3	195	11110110	F6	246
10010001	91	145	11000100	C4	196	11110111	F7	247
10010010	92	146	11000101	C5	197	11111000	F8	248
10010011	93	147	11000110	C6	198	11111001	F9	249
10010100	94	148	11000111	C7	199	11111010	FA	250
10010101	95	149	11001000	C8	200	11111011	FB	251
10010110	96	150	11001001	C9	201	11111100	FC	252
10010111	97	151	11001010	CA	202	11111101	FD	253
10011000	98	152	11001011	CB	203	11111110	FE	254
10011001	99	153	11001100	CC	204	11111111	FF	255
10011010	9A	154	11001101	CD	205			
10011011	9B	155	11001110	CE	206			

CHAPTER

Advanced Use

Connecting A Computer

Once you have DCC controlled locomotives, points, signals and block detectors, the next step is to connect them to a computer running software that can operate them. Why would you want to do that? Well, for many people railway modelling is a solitary activity for much of the time, and even if you are fortunate enough to have some friends who join you to operate your layout they aren't always there every time that you feel like running a few trains. Some people like to be engine drivers, others signalmen. The computer can take on the roles that you don't want and fill in for missing operators. If you are shunting the yard the computer can run passing mainline trains in the background.

The Railroad & Co software allows you to represent your layout and trains graphically on a computer and automate some or all of their operation through your DCC command station.

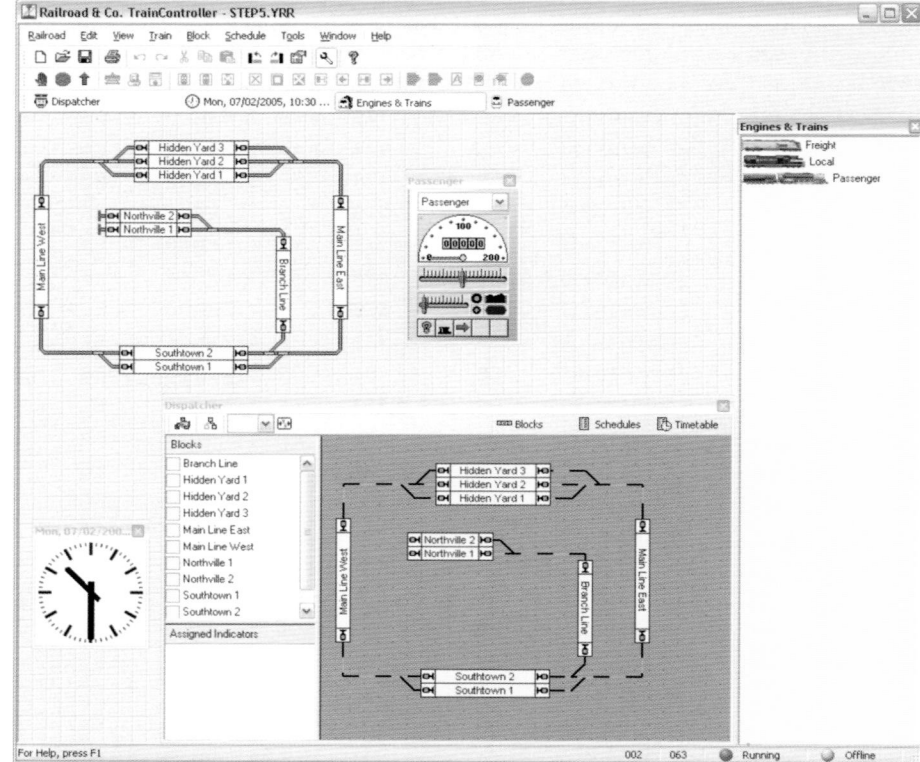

There are a number of programs available for running some or all of a DCC controlled layout from a computer. The one illustrated is Railroad & Co by Freiwald Software. To use a program such as this there are a number of requirements.

Your DCC system must support a computer interface. Some have an interface built into the command station, some have separate modules that connect to the cab bus, whilst others do not have any interface at all. If you have any potential interest in computer control then you would be well advised to select a DCC system that has some form of interface. Your chosen system must also be able to work with the program that you intend to use. Some programs are designed specially to work with particular DCC systems.

If you want the computer to be able to control points and signals for you then these will need to be operated by DCC accessory decoders. You may decide, on grounds of convenience, cost or operating pattern that some points, such as those in the locomotive depot and goods yard, will always be manually operated with the computer having control of the main line. In prototype terms the manual points would be operated by a local lever frame with the main line operated by the signalbox.

To get any worthwhile use out of the computer program it will need to know where the locomotives are. This will mean fitting block occupancy detectors to establish which tracks on the layout have a train on them. DCC block occupancy detectors normally work by detecting the current drawn by a locomotive decoder, even when the locomotive is standing still. Alternatively you can use more traditional methods such as magnets underneath the trains operating reed switches under the track or trains breaking infra-red beams.

Armed with this information the computer can send commands to the DCC command station to drive trains, change points and signals and even operate lights and sound.

Lights, Sound and Action

The availability of function outputs on most decoders has opened up a remarkable number of possibilities for animation and the creation of realistic effects.

The use of functions means that not only can locomotive lights be on regardless of the speed of the locomotive and lit according to the direction of travel but correct head and tail lighting practices can also be observed. For example, the rear lights on a locomotive shouldn't be on when it is pulling a train.

Similarly lighting can be extended to coaches, either as constant lighting fed from the track or switchable lighting controlled by a decoder. Even the orange door warning lights on modern multiple units can be made to work (as can the doors).

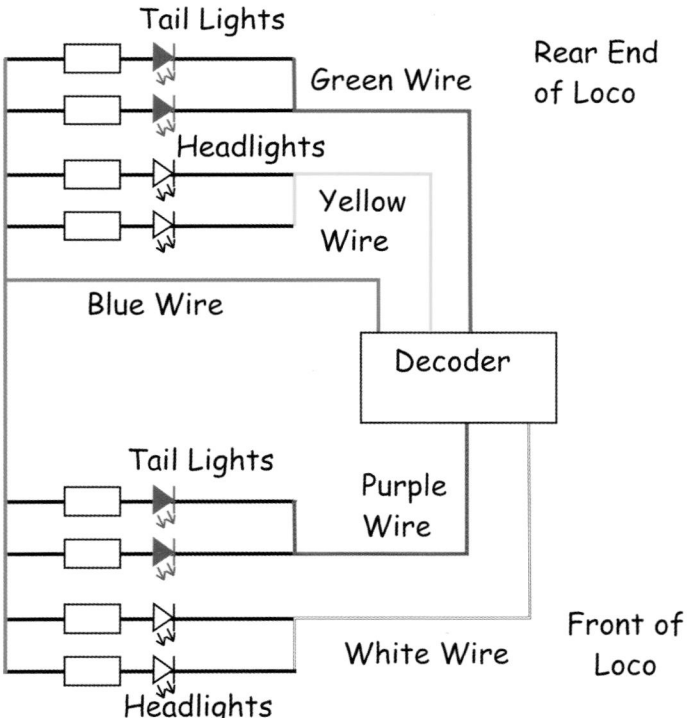

Using four functions of a locomotive decoder you can achieve independent operation of the head and tail lights at each end of a locomotive.

Using four function outputs you can have independent and prototypical control of head and tail lights on locomotives. This gives you the responsibility of changing them to match what the locomotive is doing but avoids the inconsistencies that can occur with normal directional lighting. For example, where a train is backing into a siding it would normally still be showing headlights at the front rather than change to tail lights.

Whilst it is still currently an expensive option, you can also purchase DCC decoders with sound. These enable your model locomotives to produce realistic sounds, synchronised with the movement of the loco. Most diesel sound decoders include complete start-up sequences as the loco comes to life. Typically the sounds of idling, accelerating and braking are included along with horns, whistles and other noises such as coal being shovelled into the firebox on steam locomotives.

If you have a small layout, or limited budget, you might like to fit a sound decoder underneath the layout and use DCC's consist feature to pair it with a locomotive. This would only really work with decoders that produced generic sounds rather than those matched to a specific type of locomotive.

Asymmetrical DCC

Lenz have pioneered a system that allows some measure of automatic control to be applied to DCC fitted locomotives without the need for computers. The concept is very simple; the standard DCC track voltage is made up of positive and negative voltage pulses of the same size. If the size of either the positive or negative pulse is reduced slightly this can be detected by the decoder without impairing its performance.

In its simplest form the reduction in voltage can be achieved through the use of standard diodes. These are electronic components that pass current in one direction only and drop a small amount of voltage.

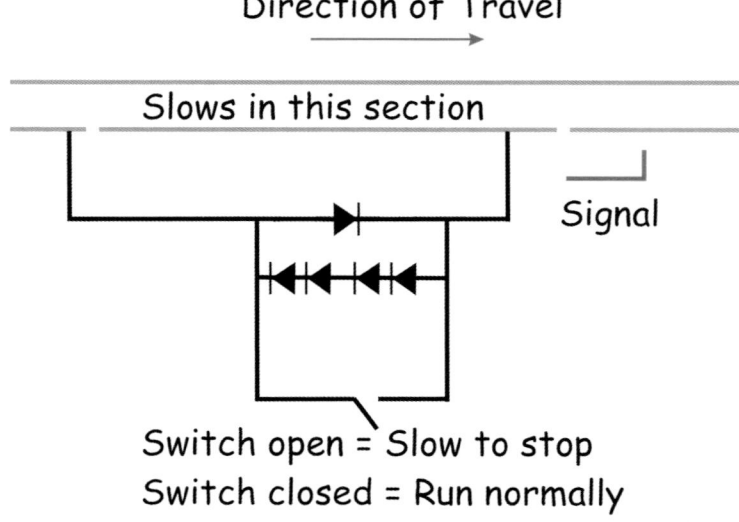

If your locomotive decoders can detect asymmetrical DCC then it is possible to create simple devices to automatically slow and stop trains at red signals.

You can build a simple unit to make trains slow and stop at red signals using five diodes and a switch. The switch should, of course, be linked in some way to the signal. With the switch open the diodes create a lower DCC voltage on the right rail than the left rail. The decoder detects this and slows the locomotive to a stop. If the switch is then closed the locomotive will accelerate back to its previous speed. If the switch is closed before the locomotive has stopped it will carry on running and accelerate back to normal speed. If the switch is closed before the train enters the braking section the unit will have no effect. It also has no effect on trains running in the opposite direction.

Lenz have three asymmetrical DCC modules in their range which provide functions for slow to stop, slow down but keep running, and one which allows you to create signal controlled blocks.

To utilise this system your decoders must not only support Asymmetrical DCC but also have CV 27 set to enable the braking operation.

Two Way Communication

It may come as a surprise to you to learn that the DCC system as described so far is a one way system: the command station sends commands to the decoders but gets no information back from them. The command station will normally issue a command several times in order to be sure that the decoder has received it, but gets no response to confirm this.

The exception to this is on the programming track. Here the command station plays a sort of electronic version of Twenty Questions to establish the current decoder settings. It sends a series of queries, such as 'Is CV 1 set to 1?', 'Is CV 1 set to 2?', 'Is CV 1 set to 3?' until the decoder sends a brief pulse to the locomotive's motor. This is picked up by the command station and it then knows what the CV setting is. This type of feedback cannot be used when programming on the main so the command station cannot know what the CV settings of any decoder are when in use on the layout.

Apart from the obvious desirability of being able to check a CV before amending it by programming 'on the main' there are a number of other situations where it would be useful to know the value of a CV.

Some newer decoders and command stations now provide for bi-directional communication where the decoder can be asked for information, or even broadcast it itself.

Perhaps the most common piece of information needed is that of the locomotive address. Whilst most people try to use a system based on the locomotive's cab number to allocate the locomotive address this works only when you can see the locomotive, or know which one it is. Where locomotives are inside engine sheds, in hidden fiddle yards or are otherwise difficult to identify then you need some other means of establishing which address to use. A special unit connected to a length of track asks any DCC fitted locomotive with bi-directional communications for its address. The decoder replies and the unit displays the address. At the time of writing only Lenz offer such a module, but competitive products will undoubtedly appear.

Taking the concept further the system could be used to provide a simulation of fuel use. The decoder could be 'refuelled' at the engine shed and then the fuel would be used up, dependent on how hard the loco is worked and how well it is driven, with an indication of fuel remaining on the operator's cab. Running out of fuel on the main could even bring the loco to a grinding halt...

Over the coming years with greater support of this technology there will be many interesting products offered that exploit it.

Build Your Own

The details of DCC are available freely to anyone who wants to make use of it. Unlike earlier command control systems which were exclusive to one manufacturer there is no secret as to how it works. This means that it is perfectly possible for individual modellers to build their own decoders, command stations or other accessories if they wish.

There is a huge amount of technical information about DCC and projects surrounding it available on the Internet. An interest in things technical is an advantage for anyone wishing to get involved in this area, but there are sufficient resources for someone with no previous electronic or computer knowledge to gain an understanding. The best place to start is to join the Model Electronic Railway Group (MERG), a society dedicated to applying electronics to solving model railway problems. They have their own range of kits for various DCC accessories from train detectors to command stations.

Glossary

A (amp)	A measure of electric current.
AC (alternating current)	Electric current that constantly changes direction.
Accessory decoder	A decoder that operates accessories such as points and signals rather than a locomotive.
Address	The number of a locomotive, comparable to a telephone number.
Analogue controller	Standard 12V DC controller, not capable of generating DCC commands.
Analogue locomotive	Standard 12V DC locomotive, not fitted with a DCC decoder.
Binary number	A number made up of bits. Values count up in twos rather than 10s. So 1 represents 1, 10 represents 2, 100 represents 4, 1000 represents 8, and so on.
Bit	Short for BINARY DIGIT. A single value of 0 or 1. A single bit can be used to indicate if something is off or on. A number of bits can be used to make a binary number.
Booster	Takes the low power digital signal from the command station and amplifies it so that it has enough power to operate locomotives and accessories. A layout may have a number of boosters in order to provide sufficient power.
Bus	Wires used to distribute power and/or information around the layout.
Cab	Unit that allows you to set the speed and direction of a locomotive. May also provide other facilities such as control of functions and programming.
Command station	The "brains" of the system. Takes information from the cabs, formats it for DCC operation and passes it as a digital signal to the booster.
Configuration variable (CV)	Address, starting voltage, acceleration rate and deceleration rate are examples of features which can be set within the locomotive decoder. This information is stored in Configuration variables.
Consist	Method of controlling several locomotives at the same time with a common address
DC (direct current)	Electric current that runs continuously in one direction.
DCC	Abbreviation for Digital Command Control
Decoder	A device that receives DCC commands and acts on them, for example to turn on a light or increase motor speed.
Extended address/ Extended addressing	Not supported by all command stations or decoders. This is a method that allows locomotive addresses from 128 to 9999 to be used.
Function	A decoder controlled switch that can be used to operate lights and other accessories.
Locomotive address	See Address
NMRA	National Model Railroad Association, North American model railroaders organisation which controls the DCC standards.
Programming	The process of setting the Configuration variables of a decoder.
Programming on the main	The ability to set Configuration variables of decoders whilst on the layout.
Programming track	A section of track, electrically isolated from the layout, used for setting and reading the Configuration Variables of a decoder.
Speed steps	The number of increments that a decoder uses to change from stop to full speed.
Walkaround controller	A handheld cab that allows the operator to move around with the locomotive that they are operating.

Troubleshooting Guide

Unable to program or read any decoders – System returns 'not found/incorrectly connected' error...

- Your wiring between the booster and programming track has too high a resistance – probably due to a bad connection or poorly soldered joint.
  You can confirm this by running wires straight from the booster unit to the programming track and attaching direct to the rails using crocodile clips.

Can run analogue (DC) locomotives but DCC installed locomotives do not respond...

- Your wiring between the booster and layout has too high a resistance – probably due to a bad connection or poorly soldered joint.
  You can confirm this by running wires straight from the booster unit to a length of track and attaching direct to the rails using crocodile clips.

All trains stop / The controller keeps on cutting out...

There is a short circuit somewhere.
- Have you run a locomotive up to a point that is set against it?
- If you can isolate sections of your layout do so to try to locate it.
- Remove the locomotives one by one to see if any of them are causing the short circuit.

The railway is taking more power than the system can supply.
- Reduce the number of locomotives and accessories in use. If this cures the problem then you need to install one or more booster units.

One locomotive will not respond to the controller...

Loco won't respond at all
- Check that you are using the correct decoder address!
- Check that there is power to the track.
  For example is the locomotive in a siding that has been isolated by a power routing point?
- Check that the short/long address bit is set correctly in the basic configuration register (CV 29)
- Check that no wires have come loose in the locomotive.
- The system is set for 128 speed step operation and the decoder does not support this mode.
- If you have changed a CV setting since the loco last worked – change it back.

Loco just stopped and now won't respond
- Is the track dirty?
- The decoder might have overheated.
  Remove the locomotive from the track and let it cool down before trying to run the locomotive again.

The headlight and other functions are controllable but it won't run... ?

- This sometimes happens when you clear a consist but for some reason the decoder misses the command. Set CV 19 to 0 to clear the consist information.
- Check that the short/long address bit is set correctly in the basic configuration register (CV 29).

The headlight won't switch on
- The command station and decoder are in different speed step modes.
- Is the headlight wired to the correct function output?
- Has the headlight bulb blown?

All locomotives behave oddly...

Locos run erratically
- Clean track thoroughly.

Some or all locomotives will not respond to the controller
- Check that all the booster stations are turned on.

All locos stop responding to the controller
- Turn the controller off. Wait a little while then turn it back on again.

One locomotive is behaving oddly...

Loco runs erratically...
- Clean loco wheels thoroughly and clean all electrical pickups.

Loco travels in the wrong direction.
- Wires to the motor brushes in the loco have been reversed. This can be corrected, without rewiring the loco, by setting bit 0 of the basic configuration register (CV 29) to 1.

Loco does not respond to function key.
- Try again. The locomotive may have been on dirty track and did not receive the command.
- Is that function valid for that locomotive and decoder?
- Check that no wires have come loose in the locomotive.

Headlight goes on and off as it changes speed.
- You are operating a loco with an older 14 step decoder in the 28 step mode.

Headlight goes off.
- Decoder has temporarily lost power and has reset itself.
- Clean track, loco wheels and electrical pick-ups.

Loco won't run on an analogue (DC) layout...

- Check that the DC mode bit is set in the basic configuration register (CV 29).
- Check that the decoder supports analogue (DC) operation.

Manufacturers and Suppliers (UK)

Bachmann
Manufacturer
Moat Way
Barwell
LE9 8EY
www.bachmann.co.uk

Branchlines
Supplier of Black Beetle motor bogies.
P.O. Box 31
Exeter
EX4 6NY
Tel/Fax: 01392 437755
Email: sales@branchlines.com

The Engine Shed
Supplier of ModelTorque re-motoring kits for Lima locomotives.
745 High Road
Leytonstone
London
E11 4QS
Tel: 020 8539 3950

Express Models
Supplier of lighting kits and Seuthe smoke units.
65 Conway Drive
Shepshed
Loughborough
LE12 9PP
Tel: 01509 829008
Fax: 01509 560878
Email:
sales@expressmodels.co.uk
www.expressmodels.co.uk

Freiwald Software
Railroad & Co software for operating DCC systems from a computer.
Kreuzberg 16 B
D-85658 Egmating
Germany
Fax: +49 8095 875381
Email: contact@freiwald.com
www.railroadandco.com

Galaxy Models
UK agent for TCS decoders.
316/318 Foxhall Road
Ipswich
Suffolk
IP3 8JB
Tel: 01473 729279
Fax: 01473 714714
www.galaxymodels.co.uk

Gaugemaster
UK importer of MRC Prodigy Advance.
Gaugemaster House
Ford Road
Arundel
BN18 0BN
Tel: 01903 884321
Fax: 01903 884377
www.gaugemaster.com

Gerry Spencer
Manufacturer of DCC conversion parts for Graham Farish locomotives.
Tel: 01476 550301
Email:
gerry@jigerspe.demon.co.uk
www. jigerspe.demon.co.uk

Hornby plc
Manufacturer
Westwood Industrial Estate
Margate
CT9 4JX
Tel: 01843 233535
www.hornby.com

Inter-City Models
Supplier of ModelTorque re-motoring kit for Lima locomotives.
9 Celtic House
Harbour Head
Porthleven
TR13 9JY
Tel/Fax: 01326 569200
www.intercitymodels.com

M G Sharp
Suppliers of Bachmann, Lenz, TCS, Digitrax, NCE & Roco DCC and Seuthe smoke units.
712 Attercliffe Road
Sheffield
Tel: 0114-244-0851
Fax: 0114-244-0434
www.mgsharp.com

MacKay Models
Importers and suppliers of Lenz
Studio 56
Embroidery Mill
Seedhill, Paisley
PA1 1TJ
Tel: 0141 887 9766
Fax: 0141 848 9486
www.mackaymodels.co.uk

Maplin Electronics Ltd.
Supplier of wire, electronic components, solder and tools.
Stores nationwide.
Tel: 0870 4296000
Fax: 0870 4296001
www.maplin.co.uk

MERG/
Model Electronic
Railway Group
Society for people interested in using electronics with model railways. Have their own range of self-build DCC items available as kits.
MERG Membership Secretary
40 Compton Avenue
Poole
Dorset
BH14 8PY
www.merg.org.uk

ModelTorque Pty.
Manufacturer of re-motoring kits for Lima locomotives.
P.O. Box 456
Blackburn
Victoria
3130
Australia
Tel: +613 9877 0222
Fax: +613 9877 9499
www.modeltorque.com

Rapid Electronics Ltd.
Supplier of wire, electronic components, solder and tools.
Severalls Lane
Colchester
CO4 5JS
Tel: 01206 751166
Fax: 01206 751188
www.rapidelectronics.co.uk

South West Digital Ltd.
Supplier of ESU Lok-Sound.
1 Savernake Road
Weston-Super-Mare
BS22 9HQ
Tel: 01934 517303
www.southwestdigital.co.uk

Sunningwell Command Control Ltd.
Supplier of Digitrax and Soundtrax.
PO Box 381
Abingdon
OX13 6YB
Tel/Fax: 01865 730455
www.scc4dcc.co.uk

Squires Model & Craft Tools
Supplier of wire, electronic components, solder and tools.
100 London Road
Bognor Regis
PO21 1DD
Tel: 01243 842424
Fax: 01243 842525

ZTC Controls Ltd
Manufacturer.
24 Chilkwell Street
Glastonbury
BA6 8DB
Tel: 0870 241 8730
Fax: 01458 837 831
www.ztccontrols.co.uk

Locomotive Decoder Quick CV Calculator

This is a quick guide to setting the locomotive address and basic configuration.

CV 1 or CV 17 & 18 Locomotive Address

Do your decoder and command station support locomotive addresses greater than 127?

If they do, is the locomotive's address greater than 127?

No – Enter the locomotive's address in CV 1

Yes – Calculate the values for CV 17 and 18 as follows:
Divide the locomotive's address by 256. Take the whole number part and enter that in CV 17.
Subtract CV 17 x 256 from the locomotive's address. Enter this value in CV 18.

CV 29 Basic Configuration Register
Start with a value of 0.
Does the locomotive need to run backwards when the cab is set to forward?

Yes - add 1

Is your command station using 28 or 128 speed steps?

Yes - add 2

Do you want to be able to run the locomotive on analogue layouts?

Yes – add 4

If your decoder and command station both support bi-directional communications, do you wish to use them?

Yes – add 8

If your decoder supports special speed tables, do you wish to use one?

Yes – add 16

If your decoder supports addresses greater than 127, is the locomotive's address greater than 127?

Yes – add 32

Set CV 29, the Basic Configuration Register to the value that you have calculated.

DCC Locomotive Record Card		
Locomotive type:	Class 24 – Blue	
Number:	5087	
DCC address:	7	
Type of decoder:	Lenz 1000E	
CV	**Value**	**Comments:**
1	7	Last digit of cab number
3	10	Acceleration
4	10	Deceleration
29	8	Analogue enabled
Notes:	Fitted Jan 06 No lighting.	

The record card overleaf can be photocopied and used to keep track of the CV settings and decoders fitted to your locomotives. This example shows the information recorded for the Bachmann Class 24 featured in Chapter 4.

DCC Locomotive Record Card

Locomotive type:	
Number:	
DCC address:	
Type of decoder:	

CV	Value	Comments:

Notes:	